I Don't Feel So Good

EMOTIONAL MASTERY FOR TEENS AND EMERGING ADULTS

JULIE A. CHRISTIANSEN

To my inner child, my teenaged self, and my young-adult self. There is so much you didn't know, and it filled your journey with twists, turns, and trouble. I'm proud of you for pushing through to a place of understanding, and I'm grateful that you had the will to change. For all the times you felt unloved, know that you are loved now. You are safe. You are held. You are HIS. And that is all that matters.

I grew up in a family that did not have good tools for expressing big feelings. My grandmother had a fiery temper and gifted her temperament to her many children. They, in turn, brought many attributes of her communication style into their parenting. As a result, we did not know how to express big feelings like anger, grief, fear, depression, hurt, guilt, or shame in ways that resolved the problems that caused those feelings. We struggled with problem solving and communication, sometimes getting it right, but often getting it wrong.

Growing up in a very strict, conservative home contributed to our communication challenges because we were taught that we should do as we were told, follow the rules, respect our elders, and never challenge authority. A whole host of other edicts were included and if they were broken, it resulted in punishment rather than discipline. We learned that big feelings were better hidden away, tucked deep inside our hearts, and whenever they got to be too much for us, we should do like that old hymn recommended: "tell it to Jesus alone".

Counselling and therapy were taboo. Mental illness was often misconstrued as demonic possession or dismissed as *madness*. Working with people with mental illness was "likely to get me killed", and psychology was taught against as "humanistic" and counter to scripture. Yet, something inside me persisted in exploring the nature of big feelings both through the study of psychology as well as my deep dives into the Word of God.

As a Registered Psychotherapist, one of the most rewarding aspects of my job is letting people know that they indeed have permission to feel, express, and work towards resolving their big feelings. My therapeutic style is very much a teaching style, and I love equipping people with the tools and skills they need to resolve their relationship problems. I often do this through the vehicle of storytelling, as that is what comes naturally to me. When working with my clients who are also believers, it is a joy to show them through the scripture that they are free to feel, express, resolve, and share their big feelings.

I use the term "big feelings" to describe those emotions that are most apt to overwhelm. Those emotions that we have difficulty naming and even more trouble expressing are *big*, and they are akin to the monsters we once feared were hiding under the bed or in the closet waiting to consume us after we drifted off to sleep. Big feelings are so common in fact, that not a day goes by in my practice that I do not have a conversation with a client about the importance of accepting, naming, and expressing their big feelings.

This book uses those methods I apply in the therapy room and partners them with scripture so that you learn the truth of how God intends for us to experience and express big feelings. Each short devotional begins with a *story*, followed by the *science* and the *scripture* that supports the *strategy* I share for expressing or resolving the big feeling.

I trust you will find God at the center of your big, messy, overwhelming feelings. I hope you will come to understand that He created you to experience them, and to realize that each emotional state you experience has a purpose. It is my prayer that through this book, you will learn how to identify and name your emotions, how to express them, and how to work toward resolving the problems that caused them.

Julie A. Christiansen

CHAPTER 1

Under Pressure

Naomi Osaka burst onto the professional tennis scene, becoming a household name when she trounced Serena Williams at the Australian Open in February of 2021. On the surface it seemed she was at the top of her game, winning matches, gaining sponsorships, and picking up endorsements.

The world was stunned when she announced she would pull out of the French Open because she was unwilling to undergo the intense media commitments associated with the tournament. Dealing with the press and their constant intrusion into her life was not what she signed up for. To preserve her mental health, the four-time Grand Slam champion bowed out.

While sports fans were still coming to terms with Osaka's brave decision, Sha' Carri Richardson made headlines for testing positive for cannabis use. This came on the heels of an amazing race and triumphant win of the 100m Olympic trial – a win Richardson pushed herself to achieve even though she had learned from a callous reporter just moments before the race that her biological mother had died. In her grief and an attempt to manage her mental health the way she knew how, she used cannabis even though she was aware that it might result in her performance not being recognized. As she suspected, the IOC banned her from competing in the 100m at the Olympics since cannabis (now legal in most states) is still considered a banned substance. Richardson's response was that she would always choose her mental health over a podium spot.

Enter Simone Biles, one of the most decorated gymnasts of our time. Often criticized by the media, Biles has shouldered a heavy burden of expectation for her continued greatness. Interesting, isn't it, that the very same people who try to tear others down expect them to be great and to exude excellence at every turn? Biles too made the choice to preserve her mental health, excluding herself from some of the Olympic competitions for which she had qualified. Biles understood that if your mental health is below peak, your body responds in kind. If she were not in peak condition, she risked sustaining severe injury should she try to compete. She was criticized and ridiculed for her choice, yet she remained resolute.

Simone, Sha' Carri, and Naomi had it exactly right. They knew that mental and physical health are inextricably intertwined. Consider that your brain is the command center for every single bodily function. Every thought, every breath, every automatic response, every flex of muscle, every movement begins with messaging to and from the brain. If you're sad, anxious, depressed, distracted, your body will respond in kind. It would be virtually impossible to achieve peak performance if you're unable to be one hundred percent focused on the task at hand.

For example, if you're sleep deprived and fatigued, you might notice a whole lot of things happening to you cognitively, emotionally, and behaviourally. You might find it hard to concentrate; you could become more forgetful or have difficulty with focus and attention. You could be more irritable and emotional, you might find you're weepier and more easily bothered, lacking in motivation, and experiencing a loss of appetite. Your body might feel sluggish, and your reaction times would be slower. If driving tired is like driving drunk, that gives you an idea of how dangerous it could be for you to go several days, weeks or months without adequate sleep. It follows then that anxiety, depression, pain, or sleep deprivation, when sustained over a long period of time could erode an athlete's ability to function at peak performance levels. Makes sense, doesn't it?

Win Some, Lose Some

Here's the thing. What good are the sponsorships, the endorsements, the trophies, or the medals if your heart is broken, your brain is fractured, or your body is wracked with anxiety? Jesus once asked, "What will it profit a man if he gains the whole world but loses his soul?" (Mark 8:36). What is the point of pursuing greatness in sport or in any area of life if the very people demanding it of you steal your joy, your peace, your very soul?

These courageous young women and others like them sent a strong, clear message. Self-care is not selfish. In the face of some big feelings (fear, anxiety, grief), they chose to take care of their mental health. They chose to respect their emotions and to meet their emotional needs rather than to pursue the pathway to greatness.

God Feels All the Things

Our God is an emotional God. He created us to have emotions as well; after all, we are created in His image. You don't have to look very far in the Bible to see that as an infinite being whose presence fills the universe, God has the biggest feelings of all! It makes sense that He would create humans to have big feelings too. What does it mean when we talk about "big feelings"? When an emotion feels so powerful, so overwhelming, so consuming that it is hard to describe it, to find words to explain it, to label it, and even more challenging to express it, that is what I call a *big feeling*.

It is highly likely that you are intimately acquainted with big feelings. Sorrow. Grief. Loneliness. Betrayal. Fear. Anxiety. Guilt. Shame. Frustration. Do any of these words resonate?

Perhaps one of the simplest ways I could explain the inherent challenge of feeling big emotions is that they often show up to indicate to us that something we need is beyond our reach. The irony of it all is that often the thing that we need presents itself by other feelings or emotional states. Comfort. Companionship. Loyalty. Safety. Security. Forgiveness. Redemption. Serenity. I would wager that many of these words resonate too.

Level Up Your Trust

The greatest strategy you can master when it comes to any area of your life in Christ, is that of trusting God. I have often said that there is a difference between faith and trust. Think of it like this, if faith in God were a video game, there would be three key levels. Level One is Believing. You might believe there is a God who intelligently designed the world and everything that is in it. You might believe that He is a powerful being who has control over everything in the universe. If you stay on this level, you will never know the meaning of the words, "tis so sweet to trust in Jesus." You believe He exists, but you don't *believe in Him*.

Level Two is Faith. Consider this description of faith from my book, *It is Well*. Faith is defined as, "a strong belief based on spiritual apprehension rather than proof", "complete trust or confidence in someone or something".[1] When I think of the word, "faith", I think of the scripture that says that those who come to God must *believe* that He is. I think also of the fact that the demons believe in God, and they tremble. Faith in God – believing that *He is,* is a good start but it isn't enough. If so, the demons would have the potential to be redeemed simply because of their faith in God. No, there must be more.

At the third level, you will find trust. Trust is "a firm belief in the reliability, truth, ability, or strength of someone or something.

Confidence, conviction, reliance, assurance. Trust is to believe that a person or thing is good, truthful, or strong. Trust is to hope. Trust is to allow someone to look after something or to use it on your behalf. Trust is to accept the truth of a statement without evidence or investigation."[2]

While Faith might be believing in something we can only conceive of but haven't yet seen, trust is an EXTENSION of faith. Some are starting out with no God consciousness – no real convictions one way or the other that God exists and that He is a rewarder of them that diligently seek Him. Others have that God consciousness, but they do not believe that God *is interested* in their lives, nor have they cultivated any kind of relationship with Him. That kind of faith is conceptual, but *trust* is the act of extending oneself further and believing with conviction that God not only IS, but that He will do what He has promised.

When you trust in God, you are **demonstrating** your faith in Him. Remember this: faith without works is dead. Trusting God is an ACT or a work of FAITH. When you trust God, you are acting on your belief in His reliability, truth, ability, and strength. You are demonstrating your belief that He is good, truthful, and strong. You are putting your hope in Him, and you place your life into His hands to look after if on your behalf. When you trust God, you are accepting the truth of His word without evidence!

In this book, we're going to explore emotions in all their glorious messiness: sadness, grief, depression, fear, anxiety, trauma, anger, guilt, and shame. We'll also look at some of the challenges we have in creating the relationships we truly want, and the role emotions play in helping us to make those relationships worthwhile. As you work through each chapter, I hope you will apply this concept of trust to the challenge of recognizing, naming, and expressing big feelings.

CHAPTER 2

Emotions Can be Messy

When my twins were about three years old, my cousin came over to babysit. She put them down for a nap then went downstairs to occupy herself while they slept. After a time, she noticed a funky smell wafting down the stairs. The odor grew stronger; she went to investigate. What she found was two little boys in the bathroom, one smearing poop all over the floor with a broom while the other watched.

"What's going on here?" She demanded.

One of the boys smiled innocently up at her. "My brother made a poop. I'm cleaning it up."

Emotions can be just like that. We think we're expressing them in the right way and in the right place, but sometimes we miss the mark like my little guy missed the inside of the toilet bowl. Then along comes someone who means well, and they try to help you "clean up" your emotional state; but they inadvertently end up creating an even bigger mess.

A third party is often required to come in, make sense of what is happening, and apply the right intervention in the right way to make things right. That non-invested, impartial third party could be a teacher, a distant relative, your youth leader, or a therapist.

You might ask, "Why would I go to therapy? I'm not *crazy*!"

Even a Broken Clock is Right Twice a Day

Here's my take on the value of therapy. Imagine you have a lovely mantle clock that is beautiful to look at, but it doesn't keep time. Its hands stay forever locked in the 1 o'clock position. If you only looked at the clock at 1 a.m. and 1 p.m., you might assume the clock is working fine. But when you check it randomly throughout the day, you notice it is not working as it was created to work.

You decide to move it to a new location. It still won't work. You shine it up, so it gleams and sparkles, but it still won't work.

You yell at the clock. Tell it to get itself together, toughen up and get back to work. It still won't work. You change the batteries. It still won't work.

You try the soft touch, speaking gently to the clock. You encourage it to start working again, to be the best that it can be. Yet, it still won't work.

See, nothing you do externally will make the clock magically start working again. You've done all you can do. There's nothing left but to reach out to an expert – a clock maker, a horologist - heart who knows and understands the inner workings of clocks. The horologist's only concern is to get the clock working again. They will go inside the clock to examine all the moving parts, find what is no longer functioning, or what is stuck, and fix it.

Wherever You Go, You Take You with You

You and I, my friend, are like that clock. Often, when we feel things aren't right, we try to make surface changes. We move to a new place, new home, new job, new relationship. But you still have those pesky emotions because wherever you go, you take you with you.

You might try to work out. Make that body shiny and new. Hey, excise is good for you, so this isn't a bad idea, but it will only do so much for your emotional state. You might colour or cut your hair, start wearing makeup, grow a beard, or otherwise alter your appearance, but emotional messes are heart-deep, not skin-deep.

You might berate yourself (or others close to you might do it for you). If anything, this will make you feel worse, and it will do nothing for your already messy emotional state. You could try positive affirmations and speak kindly to yourself. This is also good for you, and it may help somewhat, but if the root cause of the messy emotions remains, you will continue to feel less than okay.

What is needed then, is a non-invested third party, an expert in the field of emotions (enter the therapist) who can examine your inner workings, and look at all the moving and stuck parts, and walk alongside you to reach your goal of optimum mental health.

A therapist can be like a teacher, a voice of support, validation and collaboration, a mentor, or a guide. Therapists are charged with holding your heart safe as they work through your messy emotions with you. Like the meticulous care of an archeologist handling ancient treasure, they brush away the dirt and debris, piecing together whatever emotions may be broken, damaged, or stuck.

Sometimes it's just one small thing that needs to be replaced or removed to get everything running smoothly again. Sometimes more intensive repair work is needed. Either way, a therapist is your ally in your journey to wholeness.

Can I just add one thing here? I said, you are like the clock. You are *not* the clock. Clocks can break. In the physical sense it is true that humans are also breakable. We are not immortal, nor are we invincible. But having messy emotions doesn't mean you're broken. It just means you're human. Here's something else to consider. Messy emotions and the events that trigger them are a part of life. They really should not be a surprise.

All throughout the Bible we see people who were overcome

with messy emotions. Cain, so overwrought with jealousy and anger, killed his own brother[1]. Job covered himself in sackcloth and ashes sitting silently for days in his grief[2]. Job's wife was so engrossed in emotional pain that she encouraged her husband to just curse God and die[3]. Saul, Israel's first king was so insecure and dependent on the prophet Samuel that he turned to witchcraft to maintain contact with Samuel after he died[4]. David often cried out to God in despair using phrases like, "When my heart is overwhelmed..."[5] or "I walk through the valley of the shadow of death.[6]" Peter was so distressed by his betrayal of Jesus that he wept bitterly[7]. Judas was so ashamed and felt so beyond redemption that he took his own life[8]. The apostle Paul was so frustrated by the church in Galatia that he called them, "stupid"[9].

Saul's daughter Michal was so angry at David for dancing before the Lord that she threw a hissy fit[10]. David's daughter Tamar was so devastated after being raped by her brother, she lapsed into a catatonic state[11]. Her half-brother, Absalom was so overcome with the need for vengeance that he murdered his brother then lost his life trying to overthrow his father's kingdom[12].

Big, messy feelings are everywhere in the Bible. What is important is that we learn how those feelings were expressed and resolved, the good, the bad, and the ugly, weighing in equal measure the strategies that worked and those that failed.

Anyone who tells you that as a believer in God you'll never feel distressed, depressed, anxious, or overwhelmed is a liar. We were never promised a perfect life; we were promised an *abundant* one. We were not promised a valley-free life; rather, we are promised that *when* we walk through the valley of the shadow of death, God will be there with us. The rod and staff of the great shepherd will guide us. We *will* have enemies, but God will lay out a spread – a feast for kings – for us in the presence of our enemies. When our hearts are overwhelmed, we can go to the rock of our salvation. When we cry out in despair, there is a God who hears and answers.

Jesus himself told his followers that in this world they would have trouble, but not to worry because he has overcome the world.

As we move through the sections of the book, you'll find clear actionable strategies to help you express and resolve emotions, even when they're messy. Here are some key things to remember:

1. Emotions are God-given for a purpose. Remember that and stop judging yourself for being in your feelings.
2. Emotions run on a continuum from cold to hot or low to high. It helps to figure out where you land on an emotional scale so you can aptly name what you're feeling. For example, are you feeling annoyed, frustrated, irritated, mad, or livid? Those are all different degrees or intensities of anger. Figuring out *how* you feel is essential to resolving the feeling itself.
3. You're going to have to use your words! Developing and flexing your assertiveness skills will be crucial to helping you work through messy emotions.
4. Don't be ashamed or afraid to talk to a counsellor or therapist about your feelings and the events that caused them. They could be your greatest ally in achieving emotional wholeness.

Alrighty then! Now, it's time to learn, experiment, and get messy!

CHAPTER 3

You Have Choices

When it comes to emotions, sometimes they can be so big, so overwhelming, so powerful that you feel helpless to express them. It might feel easier to yell, scream, throw things, or break stuff. It might feel like all you can do is sob uncontrollably or turn your pain inward and harm yourself.

You can't do anything else in the moment; it feels like you have no choice. While it is true that all these behaviours are forms of emotional expression, by themselves, they do not bring resolution, only release. The reality is that you always have a choice when it comes to expressing your emotions.

Let me break this down for you.

1. How you feel is how you feel. Emotions are neither good nor bad; they simply are a mix of biochemistry, physiology, and neurochemical responses that correspond to the stimuli around you. If you find yourself (or others) saying things like, "Don't be mad," or "You shouldn't feel that way," that implies

judgment as though the cascade of chemistry and the ensuing physiology is within your control. The truth is you cannot control those autonomic responses to stimuli, but you can make choices about how to express your feelings. Judging yourself for how you feel only makes it worse. Accepting your feelings as legitimate and valid is the first step you can take in achieving resolution of your emotional state.

2. You can choose to act or do nothing; either way, it is still a choice. Look at this chart I call the "Thought Matrix".

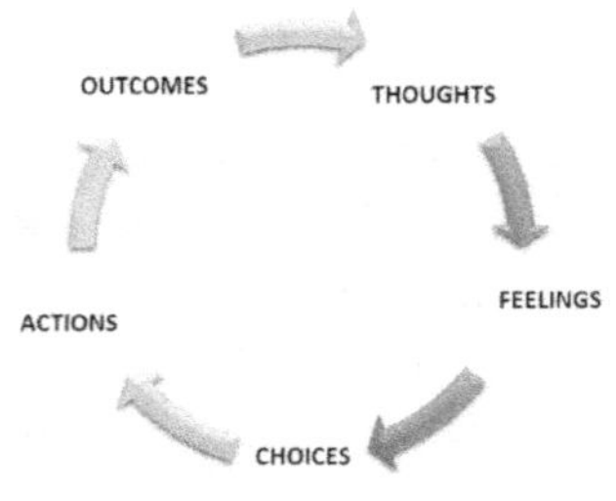

Thought Matrix

- This flowchart demonstrates the way that our thoughts impact our choices and inevitably, our outcomes. You see, the thoughts you think inform how you feel about any situation in your life.

It has been said that nothing in life has any meaning except for the meaning you give it. If you assign meaning to something you perceive as *terrible, sad, exciting,* or *beautiful,* the feeling you have about that thing will be reflective of how you have framed or assigned meaning to that thing in your mind.

Now, let's say someone calls you a mean name, and you perceive that to be an *awful* thing. It seems perfectly reasonable that you might feel *angry* or *upset* that someone said something awful about you. When big feelings like anger show up, the initial instinct is to do something (make a choice and act) that will alleviate the feeling. Should you choose to do something to satisfy your angry response, you may find the outcome is less than favourable. For example, if you choose to slap the person who said the mean thing, you might feel satisfied for the moment, but you might not feel so great when you're charged with assault, expelled from school, punished by your parents, or fired from your job.

1. Quick, spontaneous, or easy solutions to fix your feelings will usually result in a burst of pleasure or satisfaction for a moment before the longer-term consequences set in, and secondary feelings of guilt, shame, regret, or remorse take over. The way to avoid this is to be more intentional about your decision making. You have a choice in how you will respond.

2. The way to empower your choices is to think about your *desired outcome*. When you think about your desired outcome rather than your urge to fix your feelings, a funny thing happens. Your emotional state will shift. You will be able to think more clearly about the choices available to you and the possible consequences for each action, and you will make more careful and thoughtful decisions based on *what you want* rather than *how you feel*.

There are different kinds of choices that you can make. Every decision you make is one of two types: decisions that strengthen you, or decisions that weaken you. We can break these down even further into four types of decisions.

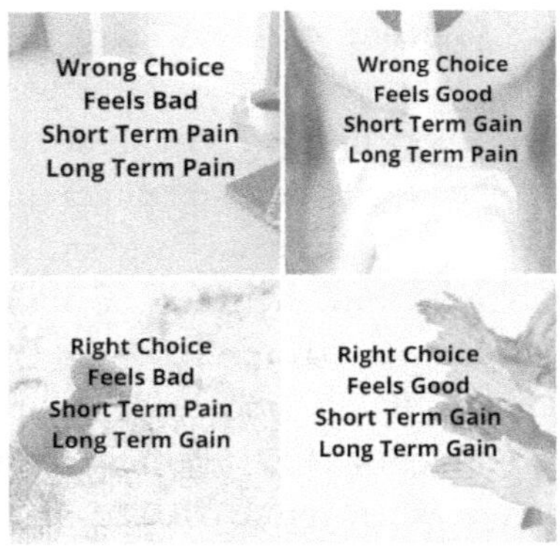

Choice Matrix

We often know what the right choice is, but we don't want to make that choice because it doesn't feel good, or we *think* it won't feel good in the moment. So, we go for what *feels good* instead. This is often the wrong choice because it brings us short-term gain (the temporary fixing of our feelings), but long-term pain, because the emotional fix isn't lasting, and the problem that caused the feeling is often still there.

When we make the wrong choice and it feels bad, we will experience both short-term and long-term pain. There is no "gain" in this scenario. The decision does not fix feelings, nor does it resolve a problem.

Sometimes we make the right choice, or the best choice available, knowing it will not feel good in the moment. Examples of this might be apologizing, admitting you're wrong, paying for something now rather than buying it on credit, or getting your car serviced regularly rather than waiting for it to break down. Typically, the feeling bad only lasts for a short time (short-term pain). Your bank account might be low until your next paycheque but in the long-term, you have gain because you won't be paying 19% interest on the cost of your car repair because you used your credit card as a quick fix. You might feel a little shame or embarrassment at having to apologize or admit that you're wrong in the moment, but the repaired relationship is a long-term gain.

The last box indicates that when we make the right choice or the best choice for the situation, *and* it feels good, you experience short-term gain (an immediate positive emotional response), as well as long-term gain. An example of this might be choosing between two job offers after weighing the options and deciding on the one that will provide you with more opportunity, better extended health benefits, or an opportunity to travel or pursue your true passions. You've evaluated the decision well enough to know that taking the job is a good choice both in the short term and the long term; hence, no pain.

This decision-making ability is a gift we were given at the point of creation. You see, when God created mankind, He gave us something that the angels in Heaven do not have, and that is the gift of free will. He gifted us with the ability to make up our own minds. Time and time again in His word, we see that He extends invitation after invitation for us to choose relationship with Him.

Choose today whom you will serve[1].
  Save yourself from this untoward generation[2].
  Work out your own salvation with fear and trembling[3].
  Behold I stand at the door and knock[4].
  Choose life[5].

This great gift extends to every aspect of your life. You can choose to act out your anger and anxiety with crying, yelling, verbal aggression, or physical aggression. You can choose to express your hurt and feelings of abandonment by lashing out or engaging in unhealthy social media interaction. You may choose to mask your feelings of insecurity by bullying others. Or, you can choose to consider your desired long-term outcomes, and make choices that are most likely to help you achieve them. Remember this as you continue to work through the following chapters. You have power. The ability to choose is your special gift. Use it wisely!

CHAPTER 4

Traumatic Experiences

She didn't want to acknowledge it. In fact, Tara* had spent the better part of several years pretending it had never happened. But the reality was that she had absent parents, both addicts: one addicted to work; the other addicted to substances. She had experienced severe emotional abuse and often feared for her life. Someone she loved had completed suicide. Through it all, she remained stoic and resolute to not succumb to the overwhelming emotions that accompanied her traumatic experiences. Suddenly, years after her turbulent life had settled, she found herself struggling with anxiety, physical responses in her body to trauma triggers that she couldn't control, and fits of emotionality. Tara's *ACEs* were the cause.

ACEs or Adverse Childhood Experiences could be events of abuse, neglect, or household challenges that happened in childhood. They can be any highly stressful experience that happened or might happen before the age of eighteen. An ACE could be a single event, or it could be several circumstances in which your safety, security, trust, or your sense of self is threatened or violated. These types of events fall into three categories:

- Abuse – physical, emotional, or sexual
- Neglect – physical or emotional
- Household Challenges such as divorce, incarcerated parent, substance use or abuse, domestic violence, or mental illness, poverty, or homelessness.

Other forms of ACES include discrimination based on race, ethnicity, gender identity or sexual orientation, religion, learning disabilities or other disabilities. It can also include poverty, racism, other violence like bullying, or witnessing violence at school or in the community, intergenerational or cultural trauma, removal into foster care, migration or immigration, bereavement/survivorship, or having adult responsibilities as a child.

The Limbic System: Your "Downstairs" Brain

ACEs can result in a toxic stress response that can best be explained like this. Make a fist with your thumb enclosed by your fingers. Imagine that this fist is a model of your brain. The outer fist, your "upstairs brain", is the cerebral cortex, or your grey matter. Your brain has two hemispheres, left and right; it also has various regions in both hemispheres called *lobes*: frontal lobes, temporal lobes, parietal lobes, and the occipital lobe. Each of these lobes are responsible for different body functions. Frontal lobes manage gross motor control, language, executive functioning, decision-making, impulse control – all your higher-order thinking. Temporal lobes manage hearing, memory, some aspects of balance. Parietal lobes manage somatic experiences like pain, and interpretation of most sensory data. Occipital lobes are where visual inputs are sent and interpreted.

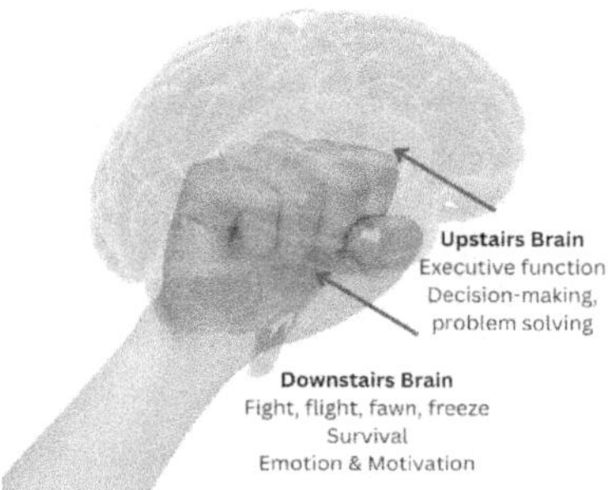

Image of the "upstairs and downstairs" brain

Your "downstairs brain" is the region represented by your thumb. This downstairs brain is the older, more reptilian part of your brain, which functions on instinct, emotion, motivation, and the need for survival. When the downstairs brain, known as *the limbic system,* gets over-activated and you get stuck in the stress response, it can disrupt your thinking, your body functions, even your genetic makeup.

Traumatic experiences including ACEs have the potential to cause you to question who you are, shattering the self. Trauma also has a way of stealing your voice. Because the limbic system is laser focused on keeping you safe, you respond to every stimulus through the lens of trauma or your ACEs.

Many people talk about overcoming trauma, but here's the thing: you cannot overcome the trauma itself – you can't overcome something that has already happened. What you can overcome is the memory of it, the stain of it, the shame of it, the pain of it. The traumatic experience will forever be a part of the fabric of your life's tapestry, but it does not have to own you, to define you, or restrict you any longer.

The Poster Boy for ACEs: Let's Talk about Joe

I can think of no better example of ACEs in the Bible than

Joseph. You will find the details of his ACEs experiences and his trauma response in Genesis 37 to 40. His early childhood experiences can be summarized like this:

- His mother died giving birth to his brother (Genesis 35:18).
- Hated by his brothers (Genesis 37:4-5, 8).
- Conspiracy to commit murder, attempted murder, kidnapping, and forcible confinement (Genesis 37:20-26).
- Victim of human trafficking (Genesis 37: 27-28 and verse 36).
- Sold into slavery (Genesis 39:1); stripped of his identity as favoured son of a wealthy homesteader to a nameless, faceless Egyptian slave. Note that even after his rise to power, the Egyptians gave him a new name, Zaphnath-Paaneah. They even gave him a wife, a daughter of an Egyptian priest – all to define him in a way that made sense for them.
- False accusations, wrongful imprisonment (Genesis 39:11-20).
- Betrayal (Genesis 40:23).

Most of these things happened before Joseph reached the age of twenty. He was seventeen years old when he was sold by his brothers, and while we do not know how much time transpired between his landing in Potiphar's house and the time he was thrown in jail, we do know that he spent at least two years in prison before he was eventually released. He was thirty years old when he was elevated to the position of Pharoah's right hand. That's 13 years of hardship.

The Key to Joe's Success

The traumatic experiences Joseph endured in his early childhood, teens, and young adulthood left their mark. Even though Joseph overcame the daunting challenges he faced, he was not left unscathed. There were three key things I identify that helped Joe to persevere.

1. He never lost sight of WHOSE he was. Remember that trauma is a shattering of the self. It causes you to doubt who you are, and to re-define yourself as something or someone different than who God created you to be. Trauma often causes you to feel like you don't belong, that no one understands, that you are alone in your pain. It causes you to forget Who you belong to. Joseph never forgot he was Israel's beloved son. He never forgot the God he had been taught to love and serve. His identity was an anchor, a touchstone that kept him grounded even in the most turbulent of times.
2. Joe trusted in God's promise. He had faith that God would work things out for good, and he demonstrated that faith by trusting in God's promise regardless of his circumstances.
3. Joe held firmly to his integrity regardless of his position as a lowly slave, a household manager, a prisoner, or a ruler.

Joseph's life is a shining example of positive acceptance in action. A term coined by Dr. Graham Price, positive acceptance says that when bad things happen, we often become distressed because we are busy wishing things were *already different* than they are.

You want the headache to be *already gone.*

You want your panic attack to *already be over.*
You want your parents to *already stop lecturing you.*

Wishing things were already different increases distress. Accepting that things are the way they are right now and forming a plan to reduce the painful stimulus or to create better outcomes in the future lessens our distress. Joseph accepted his circumstances even if he didn't like them. He accepted his present situation and worked diligently regardless of his station. He trusted in God, God was with him, and everything that he put his hand to, God caused it to prosper (Genesis 39:23). That is how he survived.

Here's the thing: Joe performed admirably despite every ACE he experienced. As an adult, having "overcome the trauma", now in a position of power, one would think that he had no reason to be affected by his past. But when he saw his brothers, he immediately felt shock, fear, anger, mistrust – all emotions he surely must have experienced in those last moments with his brothers. Genesis 42-45 tells us that Joe tested his brothers to see if they had changed. He gave them a taste of their own medicine, throwing them in prison for 3 days, and then keeping Simeon behind as a prisoner, then threatening to enslave Benjamin. He bawled his eyes out when the weight of his emotional upheaval was too heavy to bear, having to find a place to cry, then pulling himself back together so he could face them again. He wept out loud – so loudly that the Egyptians and the house of Pharoah heard him (Genesis 45:1-2).

No one can convince me that Joe was not traumatized by his ACEs, nor can anyone persuade me to believe that he was not triggered into a trauma response when he saw his brothers again. If you were Joe, tell me you wouldn't have had a moment of satisfaction seeing the men who wanted to kill you, then sold you and forgot about you bowing before you in the palace and begging for their freedom?

Oh, yeah. Joseph was a full-blooded human who had suffered untold atrocities at the hands of people who were supposed to be closest to him. Don't tell me he didn't enjoy toying with them just a little bit. Don't tell me he wasn't wrecked inside when he ran off to find a private place to cry, or when he finally revealed himself to his brothers.

See, that's why he tested them. He needed to know if they were still the same men who had so callously dealt with him as a child, if they had matured, or if they had any remorse for what they had done. He needed to know that if he told them who he was, they would not treat him the same as they had in the past. He needed to know if he could trust them now.

Truth is, Joseph could have pretended not to know them, sold them the grain, and sent them on their merry way. The bloodline still would have been saved. But that was not God's purpose for all his pain. In the end, once again, Joe remembered who he was and Whose he was. He stood firm in his identity and his integrity, and he recognized God had pre-ordained his position so he could save his family from starvation. He recognized the promise as it was being fulfilled.

I know it sounds easy and simplistic to say that overcoming the impacts of ACEs is as easy as knowing who you are and Whose you are; trusting God, and holding on to integrity, but recovering from the effects of trauma are neither simple nor easy. In the next chapter, we will look more closely at strategies we can use to minimize the effects of traumatic experiences.

CHAPTER 5

Be Like Joe

Kendra's earliest memories were of trauma. She had sought out therapy on the advice of a friend but hadn't made the connections between the impact of her ACEs and her emotional stumbling blocks as an adult. She noticed that she felt like she was a very extraverted, outgoing, exuberant person in her heart, but whenever she was confronted by a person in authority, she would retreat into herself. She often gave in to the urge to "hide away and be quiet".

When we unpacked her early traumatic memories and examined what her 'trauma brain" had learned and integrated, she realized that trauma had taught her that safety was in hiding and being silent. This response went against her God-given nature, and that is why she found it distressing. Trauma had shattered her identity and stolen her voice.

How we went about getting her identity and her voice back was a process in uncovering who God had created her to be and understanding who she was in Him. Once she discovered her identity, we then unpacked her true identity to find her God-given purpose. We used her identity statement or her, "IAM" statement to anchor her to the here and now, and to refute the lies that her trauma brain had told her.

When Joseph found himself near dead, kidnapped, trapped in a cave, only to be hauled out and sold to slave traders, he surely must have endured a shattering of his ego. He was no longer favoured son of a well-off landowner; he was victim, slave, property. During his season as a slave, he had no voice. His brothers certainly hadn't responded to his pleas for help or for mercy as he was being dragged away. The slave traders didn't care about his needs; they only cared about how much profit he could make them. His owners didn't see his worth – get this – until he let his identity shine. Joe's true identity lay not in his name – they changed that. It wasn't in the clothing he wore or the style of his hair – the Egyptians changed that too. It wasn't in the amount of money that was paid for him. It was something deeper than that. His identity had been ingrained in him from his early years. He was the son of Israel, a man who had wrestled with God, who had the physical evidence to prove it, and who had been promised that of his seed would arise a great nation. Joseph remembered the promise God had given him in his dreams. For sure there must have been times when he felt like maybe his dreams were just the result of eating too much flatbread and hummus before bed. Yet, he chose to hold on to the promise and to trust in the God of his father.

Realize Whose You Are

In the chapter on Self-Esteem, you will find some tangible steps to take towards discovering your unique identity. For now, shift your focus to Whose you are. Joseph remembered who he really belonged to. He might have been bought and sold as a commodity, but he understood that his life was securely in the hands of the God of the universe. The Bible does not tell us how he reminded himself of this fact, but we are told repeatedly that "God was with Joseph" (Genesis 39:2, 5, 2-23 and 41).

It is important that as believers in God, we take time to regularly remind ourselves of who He is. He not just the creator of the universe who sent His son to die for our sins. Looking at the nature of God will help us to feel secure in his role in our lives. Think of how the apostle Paul describes God in Acts 17:24: "God, who made the world and everything in it, since He is Lord of Heaven and earth, does not dwell in temples made with hands. Nor is He worshipped with men's hands, as though He needed anything, since He gives to all life, breath, and all things."

That same God loves you so much that He sent His only son to die for your sins so you could enter a covenant relationship with Him, one that spans the confines of space and time. Colossians 1:18-20 says, "...it pleased the Father that in Him (meaning Jesus) all the fullness should dwell, and by Him (Jesus again) to reconcile all things to Himself by Him, whether things on earth or things in heaven, having made peace through the blood of His cross."

What this means for you, is explained in the verses that follow: "And you, who were once alienated and enemies in your mind by wicked works, yet now He has reconciled in the body of His flesh through death, to present you holy, and blameless, and above reproach in His sight – if indeed you continue in the faith, grounded and steadfast, and are not moved away from the hope of the gospel which you heard..." (Colossians 1:21-23). In chapter two, the apostle Paul goes even further to describe Whose you are.

"As you therefore have received Christ Jesus the Lord, so walk in Him, rooted and built up in Him and established in the faith... In Him you were also circumcised with the circumcision made without hands, by putting off the body of the sins of the flesh... buried with Him in baptism, in which you also were raised with him through faith in the working of God, who raised Him from the dead. And you being dead in your trespasses and the uncircumcision of your flesh, He has made alive together with him having forgiven you all your trespasses, having wiped out the handwriting of requirements that was against us, which was contrary to us. And He has taken it out of the way, having nailed it to the cross."

If you have any doubt that you can be secure and trusting in the God who created you, just read through Psalm 136 or Isaiah 40 or Isaiah 43 to gain insight into the God who holds you in the hollow of his hand. Study these amazing chapters in the Bible and list at least 25 attributes of God as they relate to you. Keep that list somewhere that you can see it often. These words will give you perspective, strength, and confidence as you work to recover from the effects of your ACEs.

Trust the Process

When you've established a confidence in Whose you are, it becomes easier to demonstrate trust in His promise and purpose for your life. One of my favourite quotes is this: "Your survival rate for everything you've been through is 100%." The fact that you're still here, alive and breathing is a miracle in itself; one that cannot be denied or minimized. We have no idea how many small miracles (and big ones) occur every day without our knowledge, that have contributed to our health and well-being. Cars being re-directed in traffic. Something slowing you down in traffic so you're not speeding when you go past the hidden speed trap.

I remember some years ago trying to come to an agreement with a local physician over rental space. He wanted me to sublet some space so that he could easily refer patients to me. His other tenant insisted that I should pay the rent to him. That didn't make sense! Why pay rent twice for the same space? It became a problem, so I gave up the space. Eventually, the other tenant did as well. A year later, in a freak accident, a vehicle smashed through the storefront of that office space, striking, and fatally injuring the current tenant.

Unseen miracles happen every day. There are a million ways in which we have been protected without even knowing it. I know it feels cliched when someone says, "Everything happens for a reason", but it's true. Sometimes that reason is that there are bad people in the world who only want to cause pain, and sometimes it is that we are stupid and make dumb decisions. Often, it is that God's master plan is at play, and we have no idea how it will work out. Trusting Him is our only option if we ever want to discover the purpose for the pain.

Hold Fast to Your Integrity

What does it really mean to have integrity? Dictionary.com defines integrity as: the quality of being honest and having strong moral principles; moral uprightness. A person of integrity is honest, has strong values and lives by them, is transparent, and sincere.

Circle back to the story of Joe. There are key points in his story when he could have responded differently, but he chose to maintain his integrity. The first instance is in Genesis 39: 1-6 that we see Joseph being favoured by God after being sold to Potiphar, and his response is to manage all his master's affairs with honesty and integrity. He could have skimmed a little off the top as payback for his captivity – taken a little here and there to build himself a nest egg as part of an escape plan. Instead, he worked diligently and proved himself an honest and trustworthy servant.

The second instance occurs from verse 7 to 12 when he is accosted repeatedly by his master's wife, wanting him to engage in an illicit affair. See his response in verses 8-9. "My master does not know what is with me in the house, and he has committed all that he has to my hand. There is no one greater in this house than I, nor has he kept back anything from me but you, because you are his wife. How then can I do this great wickedness, and sin against God?" Notice that Joe doesn't ask how she can ask him to sin against his earthly master. Instead, he was continually mindful of Whose he was, and that to sleep with his master's wife would be a sin against his God. The presence of mind to acknowledge God's sovereignty in his life, along with his desire to do the right thing was what prevented him from choosing any other response but to reject her.

Thirdly, we see when Joseph was wrongfully imprisoned, he again chose to stay true to his identity. He remained honest, demonstrated his trustworthiness, and before long, he became much like an overseer in the prison – even though he was a captive himself – and once again, the Lord caused whatever he does to prosper.

The next example is when Joseph was brought before Pharoah to interpret the dreams. He maintained a humble spirit, explaining that God would give the interpretation of the dream. He didn't take the glory for himself. He didn't rail and carry on about how he had been in prison unjustly for years, nor did he refuse to interpret the dream until he had been fairly compensated for his time in jail. Rather, he interpreted the dream and advised Pharoah on how the country could survive the coming drought. When he was elevated to a princely position, he operated just as he always had done, with honesty and integrity.

Even when he is toying with his brothers, he does so with the knowledge that he has no plans to keep them in prison or to punish them for any contrived wrongdoing. Once they pass the tests he places before them, he happily and emotionally reveals all to them, again without bitterness or recrimination.

How can you hold fast to your integrity? Be clear about who you are, and Whose you are. Trust in that. Trust in God. Trust the process. Be clear about your values and what you stand for, and whenever your trauma brain tries to tell you that you should do something that goes outside of those values, you can choose if you will respond in a way that is reflective of your values or if you will succumb to responses ingrained in you by traumatic experiences.

. . .

Clarify Your Vision

Our boy Joe had an advantage that supported his intent to live with integrity. That advantage was his dreams. He had a very clear vision of who he would become even if he had no idea of how it was going to happen. It is most certain that on the morning after he had the dream about the sun, moon and stars bowing to him, someone had told him he would be assaulted, left for dead, kidnapped by his brothers, and sold to slavery, he would have laughed. Had you told him some woman would find him so attractive and so infuriatingly honest that she would accuse him of sexual assault out of spite, he might have suggested you were a bit nutty. He had no idea of the journey that would bring him to the realization of his vision, but he never lost sight of it even in the worst of his experiences.

It's time for you to clarify that vision. So, here's your homework:

1. Make that list of at least 25 qualities that describe the God who calls you His own.
2. Make a commitment to trust Him. Trust who He made you to be. Trust in the process, even when you cannot see the road ahead.
3. If you're not sure what values are most important to you, at the end of this chapter you will find a list of values. Review the list and choose the ten values that resonate most with you. Think about how you can represent those values every day in the choices you make, and then create a list of actions you can take to reflect your values.

Values Clarification Exercise

ACHIEVEMENT
BEAUTY
CHANGE
CHARITY
CONNECTEDNESS
CONTRIBUTION
CREATIVITY
DIGNITY
DISCOVERY
FAMILY
EXPERIENCE
FUN
FREEDOM
GENEROSITY
GROWTH
HAPPINESS
HARD WORK
HEALTH
HONESTY
INDEPENDENCE

INDIVIDUALITY
INFLUENCE
INTEGRITY
INTIMACY
JUSTICE
KINDNESS
KNOWLEDGE
LEADERSHIP
MASTERY
PEACE
PLEASURE
POWER
SELF-ESTEEM
SENSITIVITY
SPIRITUALITY/FAITH
SUCCESS
TEACHING
TRUTH
WINNING
OTHERS:

CHAPTER 6

Not Good Enough – Self-Esteem

Not good enough. Not worthy of love, affection, loyalty, or friendship. Undeserving. Not good enough. Not good enough. *Not good enough.*

Sometimes I wonder if every human doesn't think these self-deprecating thoughts every now and then. They are repeated almost daily in my therapy room, and every so often, I will admit they rattle around in my own head.

When I was in my teens, I aspired to be a writer. Back then I dabbled in everything. I started out with poetry and song lyrics, moving on to greeting cards, fiction, and playwriting. I wrote a children's chapter book before my twelfth birthday. My first young adult novel was completed at seventeen. Although a couple of my plays were produced and performed in my church, I still felt not good enough. My mom said I should submit my poems and stories to various kids and youth magazines. People told me I should copyright and sell my songs to Christian artists. Guess what? I didn't do any of that. None of my early work was ever published. I was too afraid of rejection to take a chance. I was afraid people would confirm what I already knew. I was not good enough.

In my young adult years, I got up the nerve to enter a poetry contest. My submission was rejected. I submitted to Homemaker's Magazine and Chatelaine. Those submissions were gracefully rejected with suggestions on how I could get my work approved for publication. Would you believe I never saw the suggestions for what they were because of the words, "not good enough" that were running on repeat in my head. I missed out on countless opportunities and buried my dreams for many years because of three simple but insidious words, "Not. Good. Enough." It was not until much later that I came to understand that my voice has value and deserves to be heard. It was then that my work was published and through it, I was able to make a difference.

These words, *not good enough* don't just show up within the context of one's abilities. They also like to make appearances in relation to body image. Too fat. Too skinny. Pimply. Hair too curly, too straight, too thick, too thin. Legs too gangly, too chunky. Voice too loud or not loud enough. Eyes, nose, cheeks, chin, chest, biceps, belly, butt... we've all got something about ourselves we wish we could change; things we believe are "not good enough".

Where Does This Self Loathing Come From?

In my generation, as children, we were taught that to be likeable, we should not say nice things about ourselves. "No one likes a braggart! When someone pays you a compliment, be humble and say *thank you*, but for goodness' sake, never acknowledge the compliment as true! You should never ever do anything to make someone feel bad about themselves, even if that means you must hide your own talent. Self-sacrifice is good for your ego. If your best friend sings off key, you should too, because your lovely voice might cause them to feel badly about their tone deafness."

That messaging inherently communicated that it was good to put yourself down. Feeling badly about yourself was somehow equated with humility, and only the most arrogant of fools waxed on about their strengths and positive attributes. While it is true that narcissism[1] and egocentrism[2] is annoying and tiresome, there is nothing wrong with acknowledging your strengths and God-given talents from a place of humility. More on this in a bit, but first let's look at another major contributor to the self-esteem struggle.

The advertising industry learned long ago that the way to sell masses of products to consumers was to make them feel like they are not good enough, and then promising they can achieve the dream of perfection if they purchase whatever product the advertiser is pushing. Skin care, makeup, clothing and accessories, contact lenses, collagen treatments, plastic surgery, gym memberships, hair styles, even academic or career choices have all been linked to self-esteem. Just think of the advertisements you see for colleges or universities, or even for the military recruitment centers. "Be the best that you can be." (Implication: You're not your best right now). Consider the prestige that comes with the title of "doctor" versus the stigma that comes with the title, "janitor". Both people provide a valuable service in a hospital setting; it could even be argued that both roles are essential when it comes to saving lives. Still, when both individuals are in the same room, one will be revered and the other ignored. This is a function of the value society has placed on social roles. Isn't it interesting that you could be perceived as having less value because of the job you do rather than the person that you are?

Social media has not made things any easier in the fight for healthy self image. Studies show that looking at social media feeds can increase feelings of isolation and depression[3]. It has long been understood that where feelings of depression increase, self-esteem decreases.

What Do You See When You Look At Yourself?

When you look at yourself do you see something beautiful that was knit together in your mother's womb, a unique creation designed by God Himself? Or do you see *not good enough?*

The vessel God created is perfectly designed for the purpose He intended for your life. My friend, Vanessa McWilliams says that she likes to walk around thinking of people as "heartbeats". She says your body is just a "meat suit" that houses your heartbeat, your spirit, your soul.

Do you recall the story of the potter's wheel (Jeremiah 18)? The potter works with clay on the wheel, his roughened hands feeling every imperfection and smoothing them out as he turns the vessel. He sees the vessel he made for your soul, and he sees perfection.

In Jeremiah 18:1-6 God says, "as the clay is in the potter's hand, so are you in my hand."

Isaiah 64:8 reads, "But now, O Lord, you are our father; we are the clay, and you our potter, and we are the work of your hand."

Also in Lamentations 4:2 Jeremiah also says, "The precious sons of Zion comparable to fine gold, how are they esteemed as earthen pitchers, the work of the hands of the potter!"

God created you according to His perfect design. Had He thought you were imperfect, He would have re-formed you before you emerged into the world. There are things that only you can do and the body, the vessel, the meat suit that He gave you is the tool through which He will fulfill His purpose for your life.

"That's all fine and good," you might say. "But how do I begin to shift my perception of myself, when for so long, all I've believed of myself is that I'm *not good enough?*"

Here's where I would encourage you to start.

1. Find a personality test that you can take – there are several free ones online but use one that is well-validated and based in science (not something you find on a social site). I highly recommend www. 16personalities.com. It is one of the most accurate

personality tests I have ever taken. This test will give you an overview of your personality traits and describe how they manifest in school, at work, in family, and in other relationships. I call this an overview of the YOU that God made you to be.

2. Take a tour through your Bible to find out who God says you are. Personally, I like to begin with Psalm 139 because it is such a powerful statement as to how loved, protected, unique, known, and valued we are by God. From there, search out other scriptures like Romans 8:15, John 3:16, 1 Peter 5:7, Jeremiah 31:3, Philippians 4:13, Romans 8:1, John 8:36, Jeremiah 29:11 and 1 Peter 2:9. Read each scripture and summarize it as sentence beginning with the words, "I am". For example, "I am loved. I am known. I have a purpose. I am unique. I am strong. I belong. I am forgiven. I am free."

3. Once you have your personality assessment results and your summaries of scripture, put them together into your personal "I AM" Statement. Keep it somewhere visible so that you can refer to it daily. Repeat it to yourself to keep you grounded against the messaging from social media, the advertising world, and the people in your life who would like you to believe that you are not good enough.

You are enough! You are a child of God, made in His image, and gifted so that you can fulfill a unique purpose. Repeat it. Believe it. Embrace it!

CHAPTER 7

Learned Helplessness

"It just doesn't seem to matter what I do," Michael lamented with a forlorn expression. "I always seem to be getting into trouble. No matter how hard I try, nothing seems to make a difference. *Nothing I do is good enough.*"

A high school senior, Michael had fallen into a pattern of experiencing big feelings and trying to soothe those feelings with substances and self-harm. His parents, who were understandably concerned about his poor choices, responded by restricting his contact with friends and limiting his freedoms. He felt as though his entire life was under a microscope and his parents and others in authority were just waiting for him to make another mistake. He was being crushed under the weight of disapproval, mistrust, guilt, and shame. Michael was suffering from an extreme case of learned helplessness.

Learned helplessness occurs when people or animals feel **helpless** to avoid negative situations. Martin Seligman first observed learned helplessness when he was doing behaviour experiments on dogs. The dogs were placed in a place where they would feel a mild but uncomfortable electric shock. At first the dogs tried to escape the discomfort by moving to a different space, but when they experienced shock in the new space and became conditioned to believe they could not escape the shocks, they became depressed and lethargic. They had learned that they were helpless.

A natural effect of learned helplessness is a combination of anxiety and depression. The anxiety arrives with the thoughts, "There is no way I can get out of this. I need relief but I don't know what else to do." Depression sets in when the anxious search for escape yields no exit doors. Negative thoughts infect your mind; "I am unable to save myself. Nothing I do works. Everything I try fails." The underlying message is that you are *not capable*.

In his audio program, *Self Esteem and Peak Performance*, celebrated author Jack Canfield remarks that the hallmarks of self-esteem are *feeling loveable* and *feeling capable*. In Michael's case, the ongoing conflict with his parents convinced him that he was not loveable, while his inability to change his circumstances supported the feelings that he was not capable.

Feelings Lie

Allow your eyes to scroll back up over the last few lines of the previous paragraph. Did you notice that the two factors contributing to self-esteem are "feeling" loveable and "feeling" capable? Here's the thing about feelings. *They lie.*

There is a reason that the wisest man ever recorded in the Bible instructs us to trust in the Lord will all our hearts, and not to rely on our feelings (Proverbs 3:5). Feelings lie. All the time. Whenever you hear yourself saying, "I don't feel like anyone cares about me. I feel so alone! I don't feel loved. I feel rejected, neglected, unworthy, useless…" whatever your brain and your heart try to convince you of, be slow to believe it. Jeremiah 17:9 tells us, "The heart is deceitful above all things, and desperately wicked: who can know it?" Just when you think that you *know* what's going on, big feelings overwhelm your heart, and it begins to lie to you.

Knowing this may make you feel helpless. Funny, that. The

truth is, understanding that your feelings lie can be quite liberating! The next time you *feel* unloved, look around. Be conscious in your efforts to challenge the feeling. Do you have a friend or five who you like to spend time with? Do you have immediate or extended family who love you? Now, that great-grandma that sends you a scratchy wool sweater ever year for Christmas – you know she loves you. If your parents truly did not care about you, do you think they would be so concerned about your choices or your outcomes? Extend that challenge further. I mean, waaaay out there, like beyond-the-universe out there. Does God love you? He says He loves you with an everlasting love, that you are precious, you are forgiven, you are free, and you are His. In fact, Proverbs 27:10 says, "When my father and my mother forsake me, then the Lord will take me up." You are loved. You are held. You are not alone. Feelings lie. But you don't have to believe them.

The Fallacy of Control and Learned Helplessness

Here's something else to consider. Michael's feeling of helplessness was exacerbated by the fact that he was focused on trying to change his *circumstances*. Do you remember what I wrote about the fallacy of control? One of the reasons we fall into the trap of learned helplessness is our tendency to believe the fallacy that we can control things that in truth, we cannot. The truth is that we have only two options when faced with circumstances outside of our control. We can either (a) change our expectations, or (b) change our behaviour. No matter how you spin it, you can control *nothing* except for these two things.

It is easy to fall into the belief that you are helpless to change your circumstances. It is essential that you keep your focus only on the things you can control and relinquish the rest to the One who has it all in His hands. This is why your faith matters. Psalm 32: 7 says, "You are my hiding place. You save me from trouble; you surround me with songs of deliverance." Psalm 56: 3 concludes, "Whenever I am afraid, I will trust in you."

In those moments of helplessness remember that you can look to the hills; it is from there that your help will come. Your "help comes from the Lord, who made heaven and earth" (Psalm 121:1-2). Remember that as God's child, you can draw near to His throne with boldness so you can access His grace, mercy and help in your time of need (Hebrews 4:16). "Do not fear anything, for I am with you; do not be afraid, for I am your God. I will strengthen you, be assured I will help you." (Isaiah 41:10)

There are steps you can take to reduce feelings of helplessness, and to combat the fallacy of control.

1. Change your expectations: sometimes we feel dejected or frustrated because we have unrealistic expectations of people or situations. When you cannot change your circumstances, you always have the option to change your expectations.

2. Change your behaviour: the definition of insanity is doing the same thing repeatedly and expecting a different result. Making a small, subtle shift in your behaviour may be all that is needed for you to see a change in your outcomes. Try waking up a half hour earlier. Spend fifteen minutes a day in prayer and meditation. Turn off your electronic devices an hour before bed. Start using a bullet journal. Ask someone who has overcome challenges similar to yours to mentor you. Start setting boundaries with your peers. Small shifts can create dramatic change!

CHAPTER 8

Anger – The Misunderstood Emotion

When I was a little girl, I had a passive personality. I infrequently experimented with assertive behaviour, but honestly, I wasn't all that good at it. The ways my family members expressed anger proved a study in extremes. Where some were highly volatile and demonstrative in expressing anger, others were extremely passive. As a child, I landed on the passive side.

In my senior years of elementary school, I found I was tired of being a pushover, crying whenever I felt upset, and never having the snappy comeback until the conflict had passed. I adopted a more passive-aggressive approach to see if I would get better outcomes in my relationships. In my attempts to discover who I was, I began acting out. I took up smoking, experimented with cannabis and alcohol, and started hanging out with a racier crowd. No surprise then, that I got in trouble a lot more. I was getting attention, and even though it was negative, it felt good. I frequently suffered intense fits of anxiety, and I began to slip into a depressive state.

I struggled with bouts of depression, evidenced mostly through my dark, despondent poetry and the subjects of my artwork. I never shared this side of myself with anyone, believing as I always did, that this was my only voice, and that no one wanted to hear what I had to say. Because I believed that my voice was insignificant, my self-worth continued to plummet, and eventually, thoughts entered my mind that it might be better to end my life than to continue living in silence.

It wasn't until I had completed my undergraduate studies and started researching anger in earnest that I realized how much of what I had been holding for years was anger. Imagine my surprise, when I recognized the ways that I had attempted to release and resolve it, and I saw how spectacular my failure had been until I found the right tools to help me finally let it go.

What You Do is Not What You Feel

Here is what I learned and expanded on with the Anger Solutions program I later developed. Anger is not what you *do*. All that acting out I did in my latter years of elementary school and throughout high school, was me *using behaviour to express what I was feeling*.

Anger is a natural emotion, one of several universally experienced and expressed emotions like happiness, sadness, and fear. No matter where you go in the world, when you see any one of those expressions on someone's face, you'll recognize the emotion behind it. Anger and aggression are not the same thing. Sometimes people use aggression to intimidate or to exert their power, but that isn't anger. What everyone likes to forget is that sometimes people use *repression* to deal with their overwhelming emotions. Consider the ostrich that hides its head in the sand when it feels fear. Sometimes people do that with their big feelings; if they pretend their emotions don't exist, they might just go away on their own. Not everyone who feels angry responds with outwardly visible behaviours.

· · ·

The Feeling of Fury

Every emotion/feeling has various levels of intensity or degrees, very much like a continuum/scale or a thermometer. For example, anger may start off *cold* as a feeling of annoyance or frustration, and gradually warm up to anger, fury and finally boil over with rage. Feelings of sadness may start as disappointed or upset and increase to distressed or depressed. Finally, feeling scared may begin as being worried, nervous, or anxious and escalate to terror.

Think of anger as an emotion you feel when your expectations are not met, your rules have been violated, or your personal or emotional safety is being threatened. The human body is a remarkable creation. With a brain more powerful than any supercomputer, and systems all working in tandem with one another, the body is a truly amazing. Consider how the body responds when you experience an anger-inducing event. When you have a thought that your rules have been violated, your brain sends a message to all the symptoms of the body, preparing it to respond. The sympathetic nervous system immediately sends a cascade of neurochemicals and hormones into action, igniting the dumping of sugar and cholesterol into the bloodstream along with adrenaline and noradrenaline, cortisol to increase energy.

Oxygen is redirected from the brain and your body's extremities, your inflammatory response is engaged, and your digestive systems deactivate; because oxygen is redirected from the brain, your upstairs brain abdicates responsibility to the downstairs brain because it is the area responsible for survival, strong emotions, and motivation. This automatic response has been coined "fight or flight", but it is more accurately described as "fight, flight, freeze, or fawn" (Source Lindsay Braman).

DOWNSTAIRS BRAIN RESPONSES

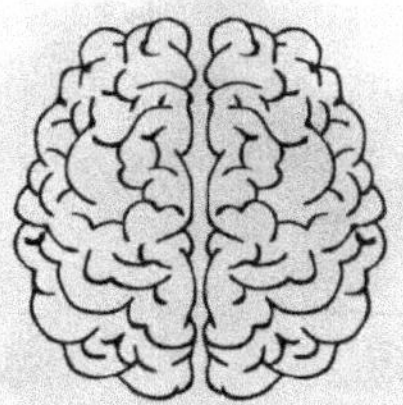

FIGHT
The brain chooses to defend itself from the perceived threat, choosing aggression as a form of self-protection

FLIGHT
The brain chooses to run, escape, or avoid the perceived threat.

FREEZE
The brain experiences a "short circuiting" of sorts, and the body appears "frozen" as the brain searches for an appropriate response to the threat.

FAWN
The brain chooses to resopnd with people pleasing, being overly agreeable, and doing whatever is possible to alleviate the threat.

The fight or flight response

You see, we all have different ways of responding to intense emotions. Some of us are driven to action. We want to run towards the danger or the threat, meeting it head on. Some of us are hard wired to run away from the danger. Others still, can be shocked into a state of immobility or physical and psychological paralysis, in which we find ourselves unable to respond to the anger stimulus in any way. Others do what they can to please the other party, to diffuse the situation by avoiding the conflict. Regardless of the way we innately choose to respond, here's the cool thing. Once the threat has passed, and the feelings of anger dissipate, the parasympathetic system works to restore all our previous autonomic functions back to baseline. How remarkable is that!

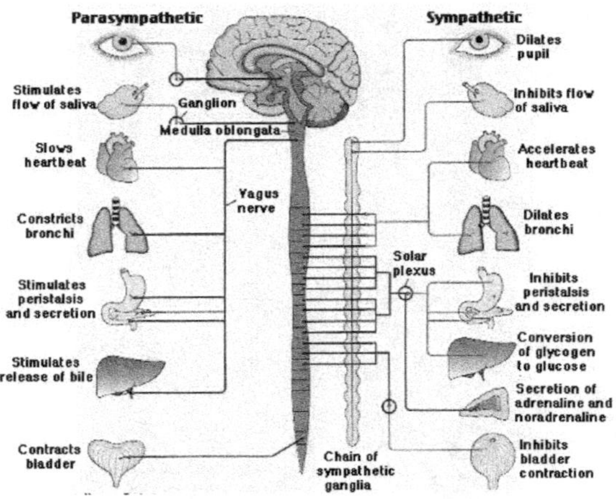

Source 1 https://corewalking.com/the-vagus-nerve/

How Does Your Anger Show Up?

In my Anger Solutions program, I describe ten unique anger styles plus a bonus style, which I'll share with you here.

The *bottler* holds transgressions, hurts, anger, and pain inside. By internalizing all of their emotions, the *bottler* keeps the peace and avoids conflict; however, the *bottler* is most likely to suffer from illnesses such as diabetes, heart disease, cancer, hypertension, migraines, insomnia, digestive problems, and more. Because the feelings are rarely released in healthy ways, the problems that cause the anger are never resolved.

The *controlled blaster* is a close cousin to the *bottler,* but the *controlled blaster* holds anger inside until they can't take the pressure. When the pressure builds, eventually they will blow, and this usually happens after the trigger for the original anger has long disappeared. This results in anger being misdirected, causing mistrust and tenuous relationships. Again, because the blast happens long after the original problem or situation has passed, the thing that caused the anger in the first place remains unresolved.

The *chronic venter* talks around issues instead of about them. They tend to complain to people who are not positioned to help, or they do this to avoid the real issue when talking to those who are able to help solve the original problem. The *chronic venter* talks a LOT, and very often others stop listening because, after all, it's the same old song. This means that nothing gets resolved, certainly not the problem that caused the anger in the first place.

The *iceberg* withdraws when they feel angry. This style is characterized by cold, icy silences, otherwise known as "the cold shoulder", and emotional withdrawal. While the other party may know that the *iceberg* is upset, they don't know why. Failed attempts to initiate conversation while the cold shoulder is in play will result in the other party withdrawing emotionally too. The problem that caused the anger will remain unsolved.

The *scrapper* tends to take his or her anger out on things or people who cannot or will not fight back. They often use this kind of aggressive response because it makes them feel powerful and in control. The thing is, it is hard to trust people who say they love you but often hurt you. When verbal or physical aggression is used in place of open, honest, assertive communication, nothing gets resolved.

The *snake* secretly plots revenge or seeks to find ways to manipulate circumstances to embarrass or frustrate the person with whom they are angry. This can show up like spreading rumours about someone, launching an anonymous social media campaign to hurt a person (cyberbullying), interfering with someone's ability to do well in sport, in academics, or at work, or simply being nice to their face, while saying mean things behind their back. This results in animosity, resentment, and more anger, and nothing gets resolved.

Captain Criticize is rarely satisfied. Nothing is ever good enough for this type of anger response. This style is characterized by blaming others for problems and the angry feelings that follow. This type of person tends to try fixing their feelings by blaming, shaming, or complaining. They never truly seek to solve the problems, only to complain about them, much like the Chronic Venter. Because their focus is on blame rather than problem solving, nothing gets resolved.

Then there is the *ACME Poster Child* or the *Atomic Bomb*. This style is characterized by responding quickly to an anger stimulus with explosive, aggressive behaviour. *The ACME Poster Child* does not need a particular trigger; *everything* is a trigger. Emotional dynamite users live in a state of heightened awareness, always ready to drop the gloves and go a couple of rounds. This style is in no way beneficial to the user or the recipients. Life with a dynamite user is unpredictable, frightening and oft unbearable. *The ACME Poster Child* may have tremendous physical control but has traded it for their lack of emotional control. In every case, this is a bad trade because, as with so many of these maladaptive styles, the trigger that sparked the anger remains an unresolved problem.

The *conductor* will attempt to take the negative energy of anger and use it to create or accomplish something positive. This could mean going for a walk, working out, cleaning up a mess, or even starting a charity or a social justice movement. Beware though, that there are negative *conductors* who work, smoke, or drink too much;

they abuse drugs or harm themselves. These are also *conductors*, but they are using their anger to create something negative. Be a positive *conductor* – combine this style with the one that follows for optimum results.

The bonus style that I'd like to introduce appears in my book, *Anger Solutions by the Book*.It is called, *the ostrich*, the most avoidant of all the styles. Like the Bottler, the *ostrich* does all they can to pretend trouble does not exist. As soon as there is a sign of problems, particularly in close relationships, the ostrich runs away, or worse, buries their head in the sand hoping that trouble will pass them by. Take careful note that this is a style of expressing *anger* and may not translate into every other aspect of an individual's life. Some people can be very assertive and forthright in certain situations but become *ostriches* when faced with their own big emotions. Because they are afraid that they may say or do the wrong thing, they opt to do nothing at all. Clearly, nothing is resolved by using this method of expression, and worse still, when one's head is buried in the sand, one cannot see the approaching danger. For this very reason, it is more likely that the very trouble they hope to avoid will find the *ostrich* sooner than later.

The *give and take* style of anger resolution is one in which anger is expressed directly in a non-threatening way. The focus is on problem solving rather than arguing or fixing angry feelings. The resolution comes about in a win-win or a fair-fair solution where everyone involved feels satisfied, if not thrilled, with the outcome. The problem that created the anger in the first place is addressed, and the best-case scenario is that the original problem is also resolved.

As you read through the various styles of expressing anger, you likely recognized yourself in more than one style. You may have also recognized some people you know and love. Often, the stye we choose is a function of where we are, who we're with, and the situation that provoked the anger. That said, you likely have a preferred style of responding when you feel angry. Keep that style in mind as you continue reading.

The Art of Self-Evaluation

Anger develops when your expectations are unmet, or your rules have been violated. Whenever an anger-inducing *event* occurs, we attach meaning to it via our internal and external perceptions, creating an *experience*. We then compare our perceived experience to our *expectations*, and if we decide that our expectations are not being met, the downstairs brain sends out a *frustration signal*.

Based on our interpretation of the events, and the degree of frustration we feel, we will respond in a manner that we believe is fitting (using one of the anger styles listed above). It is important to note that responding is not the same as reacting. Reacting is a blind response that occurs without going through the process of self-evaluation.

When we find ourselves reacting to our frustration signals, the reaction will typically go one of two ways.

1. Acting without thinking – this might be referred to as "anger OUT" – yelling, screaming, swearing, punching walls, driving erratically, or other acting out behaviours. Anger styles that correspond to anger out include the controlled blaster, the ACME poster child, Captain Criticize, and the scrapper.
2. Thinking without acting – this could be referred to as "anger IN" – internalizing our anger, brooding, stewing on it, holding back the things we'd like to say, or refusing to hold a boundary line. Anger styles that correspond to anger in include the bottler, the iceberg, the snake, the ostrich, or the chronic venter.

Neither of anger in nor anger out will yield positive results. To reach better outcomes, we need to choose *responding* over *reacting*, and we cannot achieve that goal without performing the act of self-evaluation.

THINK: This is the process of evaluating the situation and your perceptions about the events. You will also look at the possible outcomes and the options for attaining the best outcome (short term AND long term). Some questions you might consider:

- **What is happening?** Step out of your feelings for a moment and evaluate the facts of the situation.
- **What does it mean to me?** The meaning you assign to any situation will determine how you feel about it and what you will want to do next. Think carefully of what this situation means for you.
- **How do I feel about it?** Carefully evaluate your feeling state and assign a word that best describes your emotions. See the appendix for a list of feeling words that you might choose to assign to your feeling state.
- **What is my desired outcome?** How would you like this to turn out? What would be the best outcome both in the short- and the long-term? Don't just think about fixing your feelings in the now: what are the "big" things that you would like to see happen because of or in spite of this event?
- **What can I do to achieve that outcome?** Run through all the options available, even the ones that sound a little nuts.
- **What is the best thing that can happen if I act on option A, B, or C? What is the worst thing that could happen?** You need to ensure you are fully informed of the pros and cons of each action. Too often, we only focus on the worst that could happen, and we avoid the action because of fear. Sometimes, choosing to only focus on the best thing that could

happen results in making choices with horrible consequences. Consider all points of the spectrum.

- **What is the lifetime value of this event?** If this event has no lifetime value, maybe the best thing to do is to walk away and forget about it. Perhaps you need to say something to stop the situation from getting worse, but you may not need to do a full dialogue because there is no lifetime value. When the situation involves people you love, family, close friends, teachers, coaches, police, or other authority figures, you will need to be more intentional about how you proceed with your communication.

SAY: Express your feelings. Detach people from their behaviours. Stick to the issue. State your expectations.

ASK: For a response. Focus on questions that pre-suppose a positive outcome, and if possible – the outcome that is best for both parties.

The outcome that follows will be a direct result of the dialogue that ensues between you and the other party! Remember that your outcomes will be tied directly to the response you choose; so, choose carefully!

In the chapters that follow, we will look at some ways in which anger might show up, and specific strategies to help us master this unique and misunderstood emotion.

CHAPTER 9

Anger at Injustice

Wildfires. COVID19. Riots. Social and political unrest. Lockdowns. Injustice. Unfairness. Corruption. 2020 felt like it was a swirling pot of injustice that spilled over from a rolling boil. Even now, the anger and outrage that has permeated our world's consciousness continues to simmer and spit. The anxiety and sense of outrage that seems to be commonly expressed in all aspects of society are contributed to in large part by the way the media portrays current events. The more outrageous the headline, the greater the clickbait. The media (particularly social media) now magnifies injustices for ratings, clicks, likes, and shares.

How often in the last two years have you heard someone say, "People are supporting a position and they don't even know what it is." Most recently, as I write this, the "Freedom Convoy" of truckers and their supporters drove across Canada from various destinations to protest COVID19 measures for truck drivers crossing in and out of the United States. A GoFundMe page was started and quickly raised over a million dollars, topping out at just over $4 million. Joe public soon jumped on, and there was a groundswell of support.

On the surface, it seemed like a terrific cause. Many Canadians were sick of restrictions and pressure to get vaccinated, then boosted, then boosted again. They wanted restaurants to re-open and for kids to stay in school. They wanted to go to movies and concerts again. They were promised looser restrictions once we reached a critical mass of vaccinations, and then it appeared the government had reneged on its promise. There was a solid argument for increased measures representing another infringement of Canadians charter rights.

Behind the scenes, other groups were jumping on the bandwagon with their own agenda. Chatter began to surface of plots to disrupt everyday life in Ottawa, particularly in the downtown core where the protest would be staged. Plans to wreak havoc, do property damage, and to resist police were intercepted. Legitimate organizers of the protest began calling for the event to remain peaceful and for all participants to respect law and order in the city.

In the hours following the convoy's arrival in the nation's capital, stories began to leak out of what was happening on the ground. A local homeless shelter reported that their staff were being harassed by protesters demanding food. When they were told the food was for their homeless patrons, some staff were targeted for further harassment. When a security guard intervened, he was assaulted. An EMT team reported that they lost a patient in transit because motorists in the convoy blatantly refused to move their vehicles so they could get their patient to hospital. Photos emerged of people carrying Canadian flags with Nazi insignias painted on them, and others carrying confederate flags. Even then, most folks on the ground believed that the only issue being protested was vaccine mandates for truckers, and they avidly disputed anyone who suggested differently. How did this happen?

The Power of Groupthink and Social Roles

When examining the dynamics of group behaviour, social

psychologists coined the term "groupthink", and defined it as "a mode of thinking people engage in when they are deeply involved in a cohesive in-group, when the members striving for consensus allow their need for harmony in the group to supersede their motivation to realistically consider alternative courses of action" (Janis, 1982). Three precursors to groupthink were identified:

1. Cohesion of the group (the degree of togetherness within the group)
2. Structural faults in the organization (the openness or closed nature of the group also known as insulation, lack of objective leadership, lack of procedures or a set of group norms, and the sameness of group members)
3. Situational factors such as high stress from real or perceived external threats, temporary low self-esteem exacerbated by recent failures, an abundance of challenges, or moral dilemmas (Janis, 1982). An example of this is the events preceding the January 6th, 2021 assault on the US Capitol – an insular, cohesive group of people with single-minded leadership lacking in objectivity, lacking a clear direction about how they should protest, feeling defeated and wronged by election results, acted on encouragement by people in power seeking to turn the tide of the electoral process. What ensued resulted in massive property damage, personal injury, and loss of life; the repercussions of that day are still being felt.

Groupthink offers an explanation for the phenomenon of people acting more outrageously or boldly when they are in a group of like-minded individuals than they would if they were acting alone. This is how riots so easily get out of hand. Consider any protest or riot that you have seen on television in the recent past few years. As one individual or a small group of people escalates, soon that behaviour appears to move like wildfire through the crowd until everyone is worked up into a frenzy, and at the end of the day, no one is certain as to why.

Another social psychology construct that explains the mindset of authority figures is *social roles.* The most famous study of social roles is the 1971 Stanford Prison Experiment[1] in which a sample of students were chosen to act as prisoners in the study and another group was chosen as guards. The guards were given very clear rules of how they were to conduct themselves throughout the project; however, within a few hours of slipping into their roles, the "guards" began to lord it over the prisoners, treating them harshly and exploiting their authority. The "prisoners" soon began to experience symptoms of depression and anxiety, and after escalating behaviours from the guards, even begin to conspire together to 'fight back'. This study taught us that when people are placed in positions of authority, they almost immediately begin to appropriate more power for themselves, and those without the same authority keenly feel and resent the flaunting of power by those who wield it.

What can we do when big issues like racial injustice, inequality, political unrest, natural disasters, poverty, human trafficking, or inadequate health care leave us feeling helpless and without a sense of control? When life gets wild like it has been for the last several months, there are some key things to remember if sense is to be made of the chaos in the world.

Remember the Fallacy of Control

One of the key takeaways of the COVID19 pandemic season is that we humans control very little. Look at any situation in your life right now and consider what aspects of those circumstances are within your control. In every case, you will find that you only control a few key things:

- Your thoughts
- Your responses
- Your choices
- Your words: the things you say, what you ask for, and how you ask
- Your actions

This is pretty much it! You cannot control the reactions of others - not their responses, their choices, their actions, or their opinions - not any more than you could control the weather.

Here's the beautiful thing. God is in complete control. That He chooses to stand back and allow human beings to continually exercise their gift of free will is actually quite incredible. The one being with the power to control all the moving parts of the universe relinquishes choice to humankind so that when we decide to love/serve Him. It is fully our choice.

All these current events that contribute to anger, sadness, grief, and frustration – they are all within God's control. He might not be out there forcing people to do what He wants against their will, but He is certainly making His desires known. He does that through His word and the many messengers He has sent to deliver His word to us.

The Transfer of Mistrust

The challenge is that when we are mistrustful of those in authority over us, sometimes it is easy to transfer that lack of trust to God, who is the ultimate authority. How can we trust Him to be fair, righteous, and just when the people we have elected and trusted with our health, safety, liberties, and freedoms prove to be flawed, fallible, or corrupt?

We should avoid falling to the temptation to compare men to God or God to men. You see, there are certain things that God (who is without sin) cannot do.

- He cannot fail (Luke 1:37). If He never fails, we can be assured that whatever He says He will do, will be done.
- He cannot lie (Numbers 23:19) People break their promises all the time, but a God incapable of dishonesty will keep His promises every single time.
- He cannot be corrupted (Romans 1:23). God will take no bribes, has no special interest groups (not a respecter of persons), and does not value one social or ethnic group over another. This means He will always be fair, always honest, always just, and always right.

There is no comparison between God and men. Sure, we were created in His image, but we do not have His power, His omniscience, or His ability to be everywhere at once. Scripture says there is no one like Him in all the earth (Jeremiah 10:6). Whenever we try to compare God with fallible humans, we limit our understanding of His power, authority, and sovereignty.

The apostle Paul once said He wanted to *know* God and the power of his resurrection. To have that knowledge and understanding, to be that intimately acquainted with who God is, is a gift. When you understand that God cannot fail, He cannot lie, and He cannot be corrupted, you can relinquish the fallacy of control and yield your frustrations to Him.

We want so desperately to believe that we have some measure of control, to believe that we have the power to change the way things are. The great news is that you do have the power to effect change. Here are some ways you can contribute to positive change in the world.

1. **Vote.** When you are of voting age, register and vote in *every* election. This is your constitutional right, and it is how your voice is heard in the political realm.
2. **Equip yourself with reliable information.** Get knowledgeable about the issues and explore them from

all sides. Whenever you feel yourself getting drawn into a debate, a cause, or a groundswell of reactions to current events, take a step back, engage your critical thinking skills and educate yourself before you choose a side. Ask questions. Respectfully debate the responses. Don't just trust what you see or hear on the internet! Just because it's in print on the web doesn't make it true! Refuse to blindly follow one side of an argument without knowing all the facts.

3. **Raise your voice.** When you see unfairness, injustice, or inequity, call it out. This could be a little thing like someone who has been waiting in line getting passed over for a new arrival who loudly butted in. It could be filing a formal complaint to a healthcare facility that treated a patient badly because of their ethnicity or disability. Stand up to bullying behaviour when you see it at school. Befriend people who are lonely. Be kind. Volunteer in your community.

I'm reminded of the man who was seen picking up starfish on the beach and throwing them back into the sea. Someone approached him and asked why he was doing that. "There are so many starfish on the beach. You can't possibly make a difference." The man simply smiled and said, "I made a difference for *that one*." While you might not be able to make a difference on a grand scale, you can still be the change you want to see in the world by redirecting your anger and frustration into doing good for others. If you make the world a better place for even one other human being, that is enough.

Anger at Parents

Jamie and June* were fed up. Their ego-centric, narcissistic father had pushed them to the limit with his attempts to manipulate, cajole, and coerce them into being involved in his life. The problem was, whenever they were in their dad's custody, he and his new wife neglected them, denied their basic needs, and even forgot about them when at a local amusement park! June internalized her anger, hurt, betrayal, and anxiety, but Jamie was spitting mad. With no healthy outlet for his anger, he started to act out, getting into fights, and sinking into depression.

You might wonder how someone who is depressed would also act out aggressively. Seems paradoxical, doesn't it? The thing is, one of the symptoms of depression is impulsivity. When depression is fueled by anger, it isn't surprising that Jamie would have trouble controlling the impulse to fight when angry feelings overtook the sad ones.

I've heard many well-meaning teachers say that anger is a sin or that it is a "spirit". Sorry, not sorry, but they're wrong. In fact, most of the references to anger in the Bible point to God or His spirit becoming angry, and God is *incapable* of sin. If we believe that God gets angry and that He can remain sinless; and if we believe that we are created in His image to have a range of emotions including big feelings like anger, we must believe that it is normal and natural, appropriate even, for humans to feel anger. That doesn't mean that you might not sin when you're angry! Ephesians 4:26 reminds us that we can be angry and not sin. It's important to remember that the way you feel and the things you do to address the feeling are not the same.

Hebrews 4:15 tells us that Jesus understands our feelings and the things that trouble us; in fact, he was "in all points tempted like as we are, yet without sin". We saw Him happy, sad, exasperated, and yes, even angry. I can think of a couple of occasions when He expressed those feelings to his earthly parents (Luke 2:49; John 2:1-4)!

Let's review what we know about how anger develops. Anger grows when our expectations aren't met, our rules are broken, or our boundaries violated. Here's where it gets dicey. We all have expectations. Parents have expectations of their children. Children have expectations of their parents. Siblings have expectations of each other. And so on, and so on. So, while you may feel your expectations of your parents are unmet, they might be feeling upset because they believe their rules have been broken, or their boundaries violated. The only way to resolve this problem is for all parties to talk it through.

The key for Jamie and June to resolving their anger with Dad was the same one Jesus used: communication. In both recorded references of Jesus feeling exasperated with his parents, he used his words. Once Jamie and June were equipped with the right vocabulary and phrasing, they were able to set boundaries and limits with their father. Their problem-solving skills improved, and the need to internalize or act out was reduced.

Here are some tips for talking it out with your parents when you feel angry with them.

1. Think about what's happening, what it means, and why exactly you feel angry.
2. Clarify your desired outcome. Think deeper than what you want in the immediate. What kind of relationship do you want with your parents moving forward? Do you want them to trust you more? Give you more freedom? Respect your privacy? Be clear on what you want.
3. Use your words! Frame your statements so they are not accusatory (For example, I feel _____ when you ____ vs. You make me feel _____." Be sure to express your desired outcome clearly, and always take ownership of anything you might have done to create tension or conflict in the relationship.
4. Ask for help to solve the problem. Try asking, "What can I do differently to win your trust? "How can we work together to ensure this doesn't happen again?" "Can you see my point of view?" "Can you respect my perspective on this?"
5. Be willing to listen and continue the dialogue until you reach a resolution.

CHAPTER 11

Freedom in Forgiveness

Corrine had suffered much in her life. A teen pregnancy resulted in her parents forcing her to hide away and then give up her child for adoption. Her first marriage was abusive as was her second. She established a life on her own, but then an accident left her with severe chronic pain and cognitive impairments (memory, vision, balance) from a head injury. She could no longer work, and she fell into a deep depression. Her faith was her anchor, but some days even her faith was insufficient to keep her from drowning in her big feelings. I honestly believed that Corrine was permanently disabled; due to the severe nature of her impairments, I never expected her to be able to return to her job.

Then a funny thing happened. She re-established contact with her ex-husband who had gone through recovery and was now an "upstanding citizen". They started out talking about their child who had health needs, but then extended their conversations to other things. He apologized for how he had treated her in their tumultuous relationship. She chose to forgive him. "And when I did that," she exclaimed, "all my pain went away! I can sleep. I'm not depressed anymore. My mind is clearer. In fact, I'm going back to work." It was a miracle!

How a Murder Started a Movement

Dr. Everett Worthington of the Campaign for Forgiveness Research in Richmond Virginia studied the impacts of forgiveness and discovered that when we do not forgive others, each time we are reminded of the harm our bodies respond physiologically as if we were experiencing the harm for the first time. In effect, we carry the pain of the harm with us every day.

The Stanford Forgiveness Project is one of the foremost research projects dedicated to understanding the benefits of forgiveness. A 2006 study found that the experience and expression of state and trait anger decreased with the application of forgiveness. Treatment group participants also saw significant decreases in the symptoms of stress. A 2005 study demonstrated that forgiveness is something we can learn to do, and by "practicing" forgiveness, we may increase our feelings of forgiveness towards those who have offended us. Furthermore, practicing forgiveness helps us to decrease hurt and angry feelings, and will also decrease feelings of malice and estrangement. Research also shows that persons with elevated anger expression scores were able to achieve significant reductions in blood pressure, indicating that forgiveness training may be a useful tool to help some hypertensive patients who also have elevated levels of anger.

How did the Stanford Forgiveness Project come to be? Dr. Everett Worthington's mother was killed by a 17-year-old teen who had broken into her home with some of his friends. They didn't have murder on the mind, but when the elderly woman awoke and confronted the young men in her home, one of them panicked and struck her over the head. She died from the resulting head trauma. I watched Dr. Worthington share his story on public television, and my heart broke for him as he related how it was like his heart shriveled up from the bitterness and resentment that he held inside. It was only when he applied empathy by imagining himself as that 17-year-old boy that he was able to let go of his pain and forgive him. The transformation in his own life was so profound that he appealed to the government for funding to study the physiological, physical, and emotional effects of forgiveness more deeply. That is how the campaign for Forgiveness Research in Richmond Virginia was born.

Forgiveness is Not an Option

Matthew 6:14-15 says, "For if ye forgive men their trespasses, your heavenly Father will also forgive you: but if ye forgive not men their trespasses, neither will your Father forgive your trespasses." Matthew 18:35 adds, "So likewise shall my heavenly Father do also unto you, if ye *from your hearts* (emphasis mine) forgive not everyone his brother their trespasses." These are tough words, but ones we must take to heart. If we wish to receive forgiveness from our Heavenly Father, we must find a way to forgive.

The research lines up beautifully with God's word: forgiveness is the right thing to do, and for more reasons than to ensure that you too might be forgiven. Holding onto feelings of resentment and lack of forgiveness contributes to the prevalence of the stress response in your peripheral nervous system, puts you at increased risk for cardiovascular disease and other illnesses, shortens your life span, and negatively impacts your relationships. No wonder then, that Jesus implores us to forgive one another, and that throughout the New Testament, we are instructed to "love thy neighbour as thyself". In fact, it is by our love towards one another that the Word says people will recognize Christ in us! How can we show the love of God to people around us if we do not have the heart to forgive?

. . .

What Forgiveness Is Not

Too often, we are advised to "forgive and forget". Here's the thing. If you leave your house unlocked and someone sneaks in during the night, drugs you while you sleep, and extracts one of your kidneys, we can all agree that would be really bad. What would be worse is if you learned nothing from that experience and continued to leave your doors open, acting as though nothing happened. What if they come back and steal the other kidney? Boom, you're dead. Forgiveness is not about pretending nothing happened to you, but that is what is implied by "forgive and forget".

My take on forgiveness is that you release the hurt and the pain of the harm that was done. That doesn't mean you should blindly or foolishly allow the people that hurt you the opportunity to do it again. Yes, you can forgive them. No, you do not have to give them permission to commit the same offense over and over. It's called *boundaries*, and we've got a whole chapter devoted to just that, so keep reading!

Use the following questions to help leverage yourself towards forgiveness.

1. First, think quickly of the ways choosing NOT to forgive has caused you pain in the past.
2. How is being unforgiving causing you pain right now? How about in the future?
3. If you continue not to forgive others, what do you see yourself becoming five, 10 or 20 years from now?
4. How will your emotions heal once you finally forgive?
5. How can you enhance your mental state through forgiveness?
6. How will you grow spiritually if you forgive?

Forgiveness is as much for you as it is for the other person. It frees you from the emotional entanglement that you have with the situation that caused the harm in the first place, and allows you to love freely, to be compassionate, and open in relationships with yourself, with others, and with God. Remember that you have choices! Choose to forgive.

CHAPTER 12

Loss, Sadness and Grief

I was six years old when my parents decided to emigrate from Jamaica to Canada. I didn't know or understand the reasons we were leaving. All I knew was that I was leaving behind the things and the people I loved. Our house at the base of the Blue Mountains. My beloved puppy, Caesar. My friends from my church. Sure, it was exciting: flying in a plane for the first time, meeting my cousins, seeing snow for the first time. Still, I missed my dog. I missed our house. I missed the sun. I missed my friends. I missed my church. I was sad. Lonely. Missing the loss of everything familiar to me. For years after, I refused to part with anything I considered special, not ever wanting to feel that sense of loss, deprivation, and sadness ever again.

Sadness is defined as a feeling or showing **sorrow** or unhappiness (www.Miriam-Webster.com). An even clearer or more detailed definition is "an emotional pain associated with, or characterized by, feelings of disadvantage, loss, despair, **grief**, helplessness, disappointment and **sorrow**" (Wikipedia).

Sadness is a natural emotional response to loss. That loss could be material, emotional, financial, personal, or simply a perceived loss. When elicited, sadness can manifest in a multitude of ways.

Sadness impacts us emotionally, physically, and cognitively: bouts of crying, feeling numb, increased anxiety or sensitivity, wanting to be avoidant of people or places that remind us of the loss; feeling lethargic, unmotivated, or feeling physical pain (For example, tightness in the chest, headaches, pain in the throat from suppressing crying); lack of focus, difficulty making decisions, trouble sleeping, or challenges with tracking conversations.

The Inevitability of Loss

In the book of Ecclesiastes chapter 3, Solomon (reputed as the wisest man who ever walked the earth) wrote the famous words:

To everything there is a season, a time for every purpose under heaven: a time to be born, and a time to die; a time to plant, and a time to pluck what is planted; a time to kill, and a time to heal; a time to break down, and a time to build up; a time to weep, and a time to laugh; a time to mourn, and a time to dance; a time to cast away stones, and a time to gather stones; a time to embrace, and a time to refrain from embracing; a time to gain, and a time to lose; A time to keep, and a time to throw away; a time to tear, and a time to sew; a time to keep silence, and a time to speak; a time to love, and a time to hate; a time of war, and a time of peace. Ecclesiastes 3:1-8

It is said that there are two things of which every human can be sure: death and taxes. This isn't entirely true. Another thing we can be sure of is that in our lives we will have pain, and we will experience loss. It is the inevitable circle of life. We are born, we live, and we die. During the span that we are granted to live on this earth, there will be a time and a season for all the experiences Solomon listed in his famous poem. There will be times that we cry, and times we laugh. We will suffer loss and endure the accompanying pain and sadness, but we will inevitably recover and heal from our losses.

The Value of Grief

Elisabeth Kubler-Ross first suggested the "stages of grief". I would suggest that rather than thinking of the journey through these stages as a linear one, that you consider it a twisty, windy road, with lots of roundabouts that take you back to where you've already been before you can move on to where you're going.

WHAT ARE THE STAGES OF GRIEF?

Denial: When you first learn of a loss, you might find yourself in a state of shock or disbelief. It would be entirely normal to think, "This isn't happening." This typically temporary response helps you to deal with the sad and angry feelings you are likely to experience later.

Anger: As the reality off the loss sets in, you'll be staring pain right in the face. A common thought in this stage is, "It isn't fair!" It would also be normal to feel frustrated, helpless, and angry. You might feel inclined to project that anger onto other people, to God, or just at anyone who crosses your path. You may even feel angry with the person who passed away as you come to terms with feelings of abandonment.

Bargaining: In a post-pandemic world, bargaining has become a common practice as people try to process loss on a grand scale. During this stage, people wonder what they might have done differently to prevent the loss. Common thoughts are "Maybe if I had done..." and "What if..." Getting stuck in the bargaining stage might lead to deep survivor guilt. While bargaining has its place in the grief process, it is not a good place to stay for long. It is important to remember that God knows when it's our time. No amount of bargaining will change that.

Depression: Sadness deepens as you process the loss and its effect on your life. You may feel overwhelmed, regretful, and lonely. You might find yourself crying and experiencing changes in sleep and appetite. This is a typical response to loss; however, as it is unwise to stay stuck in the bargaining stage, the depression stage is not one in which to stay for too long. What is most likely is that as you come to terms with the loss, you may continue to experience bouts of deep sadness, but you will also begin to experience a wide range of other emotions like joy, happiness, and excitement again.

Acceptance: In this final grieving stage, you come to accept the loss, understanding that it can't be changed. Sadly, we cannot turn back time, nor can we alter fate. You might still feel sad, but you will be able to start moving forward with your life.

I suspect there is a divine purpose for loss, sadness, and grief in God's grand design. If God does all things well (Mark 7:37), if all things work together for the good for those who love Him (Romans 8:28), and if His way is perfect (2 Samuel 22:31; Psalm 18:30), there must be a perfect purpose for the pain we feel when we lose something or someone of value to us.

Emotional Healing

In her book *Emotional Freedom*, Dr. Judith Orloff tells us this about tears.

Tears are your body's release valve for stress, sadness, grief, anxiety, and frustration. Also, you can have tears of joy, say when a child is born or tears of relief when a difficulty has passed. Like the ocean, tears are salt water. Protectively they lubricate your eyes, remove irritants, reduce stress hormones, and they contain antibodies that fight pathogenic microbes. Our bodies produce three kinds of tears: reflex, continuous, and emotional. Each kind has different healing roles. For instance, reflex tears allow your eyes to clear out noxious particles when they're irritated by smoke or exhaust. The second kind, continuous tears, are produced regularly to keep our eyes lubricated--these contain a chemical called 'lysozyme' which functions as an anti-bacterial and protects our eyes from infection. Tears also travel to the nose through the tear duct to keep the nose moist and bacteria free. Typically, after crying, our breathing, and heart rate decrease, and we enter into a calmer biological and emotional state.

Emotional tears have special health benefits. Biochemist and 'tear expert' Dr. William Frey at the Ramsey Medical Center in Minneapolis discovered that reflex tears are 98% water, whereas emotional tears also contain stress hormones which get excreted from the body through crying. After studying the composition of tears, Dr. Frey found that emotional tears shed these hormones and other toxins which accumulate during stress. Additional studies also suggest that crying stimulates the production of endorphins, our body's natural pain killer and 'feel-good' hormones." (Source: https://drjudithorloff.com/the-healing-power-of-tears/)

The psalmist represented all this science accurately when he penned the words in Psalms 30:5, "For his anger endureth but a moment; in his favour is life: weeping may endure for a night, but joy cometh in the morning."

The value of grief is its ability to release energy that is bound to the person, object, or experience that we lost —so that energy might be re-invested. Unless we grieve, it is most likely that we get stuck in moving on as a part of us will stay linked to the past.

Grieving does not mean you have to forget. Neither does it mean you have to drown in your tears, refusing to move on from your pain. Healthy grieving enables us to remember what we lost and how important it was to us but with a fresh sense of calm, rather than blistering anguish.[1]

Another perspective is that sadness elicited by loss is proof that we loved them, that they lived, that the thing or person you lost had intrinsic value. Many times, loss is a precursor for even greater gain. Nature abhors a vacuum, and sometimes, for us to receive even greater blessings, opportunities, financial gain, or healthier, happier relationships, we must let go of what is currently taking up room in our lives.

It is true that there are times that things we highly value are ripped away from us seemingly before we were ready to let them go. We're forced or compelled to leave a place or people we love. Cars, valuables, and cash may get stolen. Trust may be betrayed. Privacy may be breached. Freedoms may be stripped away. People may be unfairly terminated from their jobs. Money might run out. Status could be lost. The principles of the inevitability of pain and the value of grief remain consistent; even when what happens appears to be unfair, we can choose how we will perceive the loss and its meaning in our lives.

Remember our friend Joe, who lost his freedom, his status, his family, his home, and his identity. Even in all of that, there was purpose in the loss. He channelled his grief and sadness into remembering the promise, remembering who and Whose he was, and standing in his integrity.

It's okay to feel sad. It's okay to cry about the loss. Joe cried. Bawled out loud so the whole household could hear. When the wives of David and his army were taken into captivity, they all wept aloud. When Bathsheba and David's infant child died, he mourned openly. Jesus wept at Lazarus's grave. It's okay to express your grief. It's *right* to express your grief.

The Importance of Ritual

Wakes, funerals, celebrations of life, homegoing services, candle-light vigils, are all rituals that help us to express and resolve our grief. Rituals allow us to find closure, to express our pain in the presence of others who share the loss, to find a sense of community in the loss, and to say our farewells to the one we lost.

For those who have lost a loved one during the COVID-19 pandemic, the experience of loss and the subsequent grief has been an isolating and lonely one. On top of perhaps losing the regularity of work, kids losing out on classroom and playground time with friends, losing gym time, girls' nights, birthday parties, and a host of other community gatherings that were "cancelled" by COVID, it doesn't sit right with people that their loved ones died in hospital without their family close because of restrictions.

Funeral services were limited so that only "people who made it onto the list" were allowed to pay their respects in person. Burials and graveside ceremonies were postponed until people could meet up in person. After-service gatherings were limited. People couldn't hug to express their common grief. They couldn't linger to share stories, or just be present with one another as a community who experienced a collective loss because the funeral homes had to disinfect the premises before the next group came in. The lack of access to traditional rituals through which we could express our grief, in effect, became another loss.

It is no wonder then, that people are sadder, or that mental health is suffering during these COVID times. Loneliness, loss, sadness, and grief are the markers of the global pandemic.

Hope Among the Ruins

Remember King Solomon's famous poem? We have hope that even though we go through seasons of loss, pain, grief, and sadness, no season lasts forever! There is a time to weep, but there will also come again, a time to laugh. There is a time to mourn, but there will also come a time for dancing. One of my favourite Bible verses applies here: "Weeping may endure for a night, but joy comes in the morning" (Psalm 30: 5).

Loss often causes us to feel as though the world as we know it is crumbling around our feet. Even in a world of restrictions, masking mandates, remote funerals, graduations, and weddings, we can still find ways to use rituals to help us heal from our losses. Here are three rituals you can incorporate into your grieving process to help you unpack your sadness and express it in a healthy way.

1. **Write a letter to the person, pet, friendship, love, or thing that you lost. List the reasons it was special and important to you**. Share how that thing brough joy, light, laughter, or value to your life. Express the reasons why you will miss it. List the ways in which you will honour the place that the thing/person you lost had in your life. Say your goodbyes and share how the memory of their value will live on inside of you.

2. **Get some floating candles** (you can find biodegradable floating paper lanterns or floating candles made of natural substances like soy or beeswax that won't negatively impact our waterways). Go to the banks of a body of water (river or lake). Make a ritual of lighting candles that represent the thing or person you lost. Pronounce some words over it, sing, recite a poem – whatever helps you to feel as though you are properly honouring the memory of what was lost – then light the candles and set them afloat on the water.

3. **Use your journal** to process your grief and to remind yourself of how having that person or thing in your life made it richer, and you can take the richness of those experiences with you.

Remember that healthy grieving is marked by a reduction of pain and a sense of peace. While you may continue to feel the absence of what you lost, you can find peace and comfort, even joy in the memory of how your life was better because of that thing; and knowing that where one door closes, another opens. Remember too, that rituals don't have to be a "one and done" event. You can return to rituals when you need them. Give yourself quiet space and time to journal, reflect, and cry. Write an "I miss you" letter. Go to a Catholic church even if you're not Catholic and light a candle for your lost loved one. Seek out opportunities in your community to volunteer or meet up with friends who also share the loss for a night of camaraderie. These are all healthy ways to express your sadness and to resolve your grief. Weeping may endure for a night, but joy comes in the morning.

CHAPTER 13

Fear (Not) – A 365-Day Command

Years ago, our youth group and music team travelled in a multi-vehicle caravan from Ontario to Newfoundland, crossing four provinces and a span of Atlantic Ocean, all to assist in providing music ministry for a church group's annual camp meeting. We had a fabulous time, and on our way out of Grand Falls-Windsor, Newfoundland, one of the men who was on the trip with us suggested we stop for a short hike. Curiosity got the better of us, so we agreed. He said, "It's not a long hike, but you will really love what you see when we get there, and it's a surprise."

Okayyyyy. It isn't every day that you're invited to take a group of teenagers and young adults into some unknown woods off an un-marked road in the middle of Nowhere, Newfoundland, led by a man who won't say anything except, "Trust me; it's a surprise."

Kind of sounds like a premise for a horror flick, doesn't it?

So, we tromped about 5 minutes on a dirt trail, and then we came across a fresh paw print. FRESH. He glanced at it and said, "Oh! A bear has just been through here."

A bear.

Right.

This was about the time that some of us, me included, started to wonder aloud if this "surprise" hiking trip was such a great idea. I mean, there was still water in the indent where the bear had left its track. I was rather feeling like returning to our vehicles would be a very good idea. The prickly feeling at the backs of our necks, the increased heart rate, and the feeling of our blood running cold when we thought of a bear being loose in the same woods we were disturbing, was no other feeling than *fear*.

Fear is defined as "an unpleasant emotion caused by the belief that someone or something is dangerous, likely to cause pain, or a threat" (Dictionary.com). Over the last two years, we have seen an explosion of fear in the zeitgeist. Fear of the virus. Fear of the vaccine. Fear of climate change. Fear of the restrictions. Fear from the easing of restrictions. Fear for our children. Fear of public spaces. Fear of isolation. Fear of the police. Fear of the government. Fear of politicians and their intentions. Fear of protests and uprisings. Even with all the recalls of late, there has been a growing fear of food.

Fear is a Powerful Motivator

Just as anger is given to us for a reason, so is fear. Fear alerts us to danger and encourages us to respond appropriately. It evokes a physiological response originating in the limbic system, that is closely related to anger (except where body temperature runs hot with anger, it runs cold with fear). Like anger, fear is a universally experienced and expressed emotion, one that alerts us to danger, and prompts our survival instinct to do what is necessary to keep us safe. In that way, fear can be a powerful motivator. Fear may compel us to flee from a situation (For example, evacuating a community threatened by forest fires or swerving a vehicle to avoid striking a moose). It may also motivate us to push ahead and fight (For example, riding out to battle to confront the enemy). At other times, fear may cause us to freeze (For example, stand in shock, unable to respond while watching a train wreck), or fawn (For example, give in to a bully who is threatening our safety if we won't share our lunch). In almost every case, the underlying belief is that by taking some form of action, we decrease the level of threat. Once the danger is passed, our fear response should subside.

Fear is Contextual

Most of the time, when the emotion of fear is ignited, there is a tangible reason. Remember the definition of fear: it is an uncomfortable or unpleasant feeling that emerges from the belief or perception that someone or something may be dangerous, painful, or threatening.

Fear has a context. Hiking through the woods and coming upon fresh bear tracks and still-steaming scat: the fear that evokes is real *and* founded. Fear does not typically show up in the absence of a fear-inducing stimulus. In other words, nine times out of ten, if you are experiencing fear, you have a good reason.

We are also admonished that we have not received the *"spirit of bondage* again to fear"; rather, we have been given the "spirit of adoption" so we can run to God and call him, "Daddy" (Romans 8:15). The word picture this verse evokes for me is the image of a small child in a thunderstorm running to his father because he is afraid of the thunder and lightning. He doesn't have to think twice, he just runs to daddy. In that same way, we can run to our Heavenly Father whenever we feel afraid.

Fear is No Hindrance for God

The command, "fear not" appears 365 times in the Bible. Many say that this is an everyday reminder that we need not be afraid. This does not mean that we should never *feel* fear; it means that we should not allow ourselves to be *overcome* by fear. Think about this. When the Israelites were at the Red Sea, trapped in a kill box between a body of water, a mountain pass, and Pharoah's army, they were terrified and in a state of mass panic. When the disciples were in a boat with Jesus on the Sea of Galilea and a storm threatened to overturn the boat, they were absolutely afraid. When the disciples were hiding away from the Jews after Jesus had been crucified, they were huddled together in fear (John 20:19). Yet in every situation where fear abounded, God's miraculous power did much more abound! It is arguable that God does some of His best work when fear is present.

God is not impeded by your fear. He is not hindered by anything – He is all powerful, after all. What He *wants* is for you to trust Him despite your fear. When you are feeling fearful, that is a perfect time to level up from faith to trust. Psalm 56: 3-4 says, "Whenever I am afraid, I will trust in you. I have put my trust in God; I will not fear what flesh can do to me *(translation mine)*." Verse 9 continues, "When I cry out to you, then my enemies will turn back: this I know; for God is for me." Verse 11 repeats David's assertion of his trust in God. "In God, I have put my trust; I will not be afraid of what men can do to me."

Even when fear compels us to flee, God is there. Psalm 46:1 declares that God is our refuge and strength, a present help in times of trouble." Psalm 32:7 says, "You are my hiding place; you will preserve me from trouble. You will surround me with songs of deliverance." This verse concludes with the word, "Selah", which means, *let that sink in. Soak it up.* If you're looking for a place to hide, to retreat from the things in life that threaten you physically, spiritually, or emotionally, look no further. The name of the Lord is our strong tower that we can run to and feel safe (Proverbs 18:10).

What strategies can we use when we find ourselves confronted with real or perceived danger?

Think it Through

Remember the thought matrix and the importance of waging war on the battlefield of the mind? We can do the same when it comes to fear; after all, fear often grows out of our thoughts and the meaning we attach to the stimuli around us. When you find yourself feeling fearful of something in the future, ask yourself these questions:

1. Is it possible? Could the thing you fear actually come to pass?
2. Is it plausible? Look, anything is possible, so if you answer 'yes' to the first question and stop there, you will remain trapped in fear. But asking if an eventuality is plausible gets you thinking about the likelihood that it will happen.
3. What can I do to prevent this from happening? If the danger is real (For example, high winds could damage my home), what can I do to mitigate the damage?
4. How can I prepare for what is likely to happen? How might I prepare for any unforeseen contingencies? How can I prepare for the worst while planning and hoping for the best of outcomes?

Using these questions as a guide, you can begin to redirect your thoughts away from the paralysis of fear toward the proactive response that has the best probability of helping you achieve your desired outcomes. It will serve you well to remember that once you have done all you can to protect yourself against danger, the God of the universe is standing by, waiting with open arms for you to run to Him saying, "Daddy, I'm scared." He will be your strong tower and your hiding place. With your trust securely in Him, you can be afraid *and* know that He has got everything under His control.

CHAPTER 14

Be Anxious for Nothing

For Sandra, it showed up as full-body tremors, heart palpitations, and tingling in her hands and feet. For James, it was the inability to relax, headaches, and an upset stomach. For Nadine, it showed up in the form of nosebleeds and a form of insomnia. For Nico, it was the overwhelming need to avoid places, people, or situations. Although it may manifest in a myriad of ways, anxiety can severely disrupt your plans and your life.

The Beck Anxiety Inventory is a tool commonly used by therapists to measure 21 typical symptoms of anxiety and their severity. The list includes numbness, tingling, flushed skin, sweating, cold hands, confusion, irritability, difficulty sleeping, fear of the worst, and an overwhelming feeling of dread.

Certainly, there are situations and events in our lives that can be anxiety provoking. That first job interview. Applying for university or college. Studying for SATS, MSATS, or LSATS. Asking someone out on a date. Purchasing your first vehicle. That first plane ride. Taking your driver's test.

Our bodies are built to handle short bursts of anxiety. The

sympathetic nervous system responds to anxiety invoking situations or stimuli by activating the limbic system (downstairs brain responsible for the fight, flight, freeze, or fawn response), and triggering a cascade of hormonal and neurochemical activity. This results in pupil dilation, an increase in cholesterol and sugar production, re-direction of certain bodily functions including blood flow and oxygen distribution, an increase of cortisol, epinephrine, and adrenaline being released into the blood, and lactic acid into muscles in preparation for flight or flight. When the anxious moment passes, the body should return to baseline or normal functions.

When anxiety is persistent and unrelenting, the body doesn't have time to rest or return to baseline. It continues to produce those stress-responding neurochemicals and hormones, creating added strain on the body. Where fear is a natural response to a perceived danger or threat, anxiety is the body's natural response to stress. Some levels of anxiety coupled with fear are appropriate within the right context; however, if those feelings of anxiety are extreme, or they persist for longer than six months, and they are interfering with your life, you may be dealing with an anxiety disorder.

Anxiety Doesn't Care

Unlike fear, which is primarily contextual, anxiety doesn't much care what is going on in your life. It doesn't care how rich or powerful you are; it doesn't care if you are deliriously happy in your new relationship or that recent promotion. It doesn't care that you have a clean driving record, or that your favourite place is on the beach on some secluded island. And it certainly doesn't care if its arrival on the scene is inconvenient for you.

Anxiety shows up in the board room, on the stage, in the halls of power. It shows up when you're having fun with your friends or your date, and in the middle of that presentation you're making to your high-profile client. It shows up while you're sleeping, when you're on a road trip, or just as you settle into your seat in business class. It shows up whenever it feels like it. It simply doesn't care.

A Study in Social Anxiety: The Insecure King

The Bible has no end of stories of people who struggled with anxiety. Sometimes that anxiety was short-lived; in other cases, it was persistent and distressing.

King Saul likely suffered from what would be recognized today as a form of social anxiety. The National Institute of Mental Health describes social anxiety as "an intense, persistent fear of being watched and judged by others." Saul's anxiety was most certainly rooted in his low self-esteem, insecurity, and a fear of *not being good enough* (hey, does that sound familiar?).

1 Samuel 15 tells the story of Saul having disobeyed the prophet, then lying to cover up his mistakes, saying in verse 24, "I feared the people". He feared the people because he was desperate for approval. Consider that prior to being anointed the first king of Israel, he was just a regular "Joe", albeit taller-than-typical, and he had been thrust into a leadership role that had never existed before. It appears he not been adequately prepared for being king over a great people. How do you prepare for a job no one has ever held before? Then, David came along and gained a reputation as a fierce warrior, one even more feared than Saul; it is no wonder jealously consumed him much that he attempted to murder David several times. All because he needed the approval of the people. Sadly, Saul's anxiety contributed to his downfall. The more anxious he became, the poorer decisions he made, ultimately leading to him losing his kingdom to David, the death of almost his entire family, and his suicide on the battlefield.

Luke 12:22-32 says, "Take no thought for your life, what you will eat, not for your body or your clothing... Seek ye first the kingdom of God and his righteousness, and all these things will be added to you.

Philippians 4:6 instructs us to "Be careful for nothing; but in every thing by prayer and supplication with thanksgiving let your requests be made known unto God."

Anxiety is Burdensome

Is it any wonder that anxiety often feels like a heavy weight? It's not a coincidence that anxiety and depression often appear together in people struggling with mental health issues. Anxiety is burdensome. It is intrusive and interfering – anxiety meddles. Consider the nature of anxiety: it shows up whenever it feels like; it doesn't care who you are, about your social status or your wealth. It creates feelings of panic so strong that sometimes people fear they might be dying. The embarrassment and shame of having a panic attack often creates a secondary anxiety, which contributes to social anxiety and fear of certain situations in which a panic attack might occur. So, now anxiety is interfering with going out with friends, attending church, participating in sports, driving, flying and other activities because of a single thought, "What if I have a panic attack?"

1 Peter 5:7 recognizes that anxiety is a burden and encourages us to cast all our cares on Christ because He cares for us. Matt 11:30 encourages us to approach Jesus with our burdens and trade them for His yoke, which is easy compared to the weights we carry. The author of the book of Hebrews also encouraged us to set aside every weight that so easily burdens us down, and to run the race (of life) with patience, looking to Jesus who already knows how things are going to work out for us (Hebrews 12:1-2).

. . .

We Have Choices

Sai Baba said, "All action results from thought, so it is thoughts that matter." You have the choice to entertain anxious thoughts or to re-direct them. Shifts in thought do not have to be big, but they must be significant. You can start with a simple question like:

1. Does this thought empower or limit me?
2. What if I looked at this situation through someone else's eyes?
3. What if I could generate the outcomes I want without any negative fallout?

Remember, belief is the basis of action; it follows then, that to effect any changes to an anxious state, limiting beliefs must be challenged. William Glasser coined the term "self-evaluation" to explain the art of always examining our actions and asking ourselves questions. Some useful questions to ask when feeling overcome with anxiety:

1. Is this thought making me feel good or bad?
2. Is this thought event true?
3. What is my desired outcome beyond wanting my immediate anxious feelings to go away?
4. Will I get closer to or further away from my desired outcomes by entertaining this anxious thought or belief?

This self evaluation process helps to pull your brain out of autopilot; rather, actively exploring your thoughts and challenging will help you to consciously work towards achieving more positive outcomes both in the short and long term.

Circle Back to The CHOICE Matrix

Remember the quadrant in the Choice Matrix of short-term gain/long-term pain? Anxiety doesn't feel good. In fact, it feels downright awful. Pounding heart, racing thoughts, shakiness and trembling, light-headedness, sweating, dry mouth – anxiety feels terrible. Freud's "hedonic principle" says that humans will always do more to avoid pain than we will to gain pleasure. Always. When caught in the throes of an anxiety attack the temptation will inevitably arise to just "fix the feeling" – to do something that will make the anxiety go away. The natural choice would be avoidance.

Flight or avoidance might feel great in the short-term, but it may create greater problems in the long-term, and here's why. Avoidance is self-reinforcing. What this means is that when you feel anxious, if you respond with avoidance and the anxiety abates as a result, you will feel better (therefore reinforcing your avoidant behaviour). That may be all fine and good for the moment, but if you continue to choose avoidance to manage anxiety, your solution will quickly become the problem, creating long-term pain. Likewise, other short-term fixes like using drugs, painkillers, alcohol, or other risky behaviours might provide an immediate solution, but they will eventually become an even greater problem – one more challenging to overcome.

What to do, then, when you catch yourself leaning toward a quick fix? Here's a template you can use to help you shift your thoughts and emotional state through intentional action.

Aware: Direct your awareness to what you are doing in the moment (handwringing, biting nails, fidgeting, avoidance, or other self-soothing behaviours)

Acknowledge: "I see that I'm wringing my hands again." "I notice myself leaning towards avoiding going out with my friends."

Accept: Be okay with your current behaviour. Don't judge it. Do not blame, shame, or complain about your actions. If you can accept the behaviour while acknowledging that you want to change it, you can then plan how you will move toward change or what you will do instead. Try to do this all without judgement.

Assess: "How am I *feeling* in this moment? Am I anxious? Nervous? Bored? Lonely? Sad? Tired?" AM I just doing this out of habit? If I am trying to fix a feeling, what might I do instead that would have more effectiveness? IS there something I am thinking that is contributing to this feeling? IF I shift my thoughts, might the feeling change? If the feelings change, it is likely that my anxious behaviours will stop.

Amend: Actively embark on extinguishing the old behaviour and introducing a healthier choice.

How Will I Know?

Coping with anxiety and managing anxious thoughts can often seem like an ongoing battle with a lot of gaining ground only to lose it again. You might be wondering how you can measure if you are truly seeing a shift in your anxious states after applying a coping strategy or two.

One of the tools I often use in my practice is a chart that measures the degree to which you are feeling anxious or distressed. The measurements are called "Subjective Units of Distress" or SUDs. The SUD Scale helps to conceptualize the intensity of a feeling using a numerical rating scale.

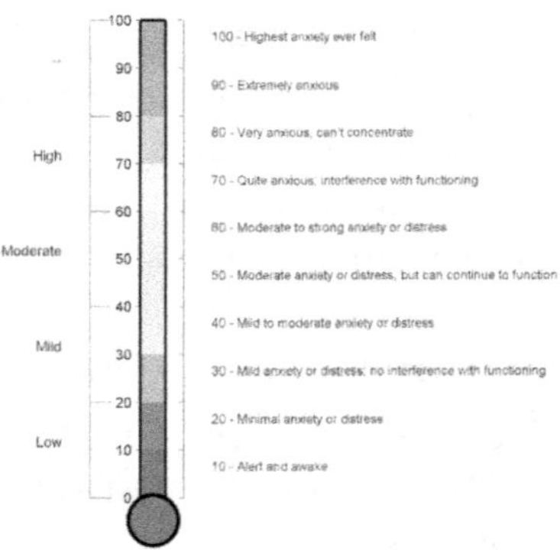

The Subjective Units of Distress Scale

How to Use the SUD Scale

1. Begin by measuring your current level of distress. Document your current SUD score.
2. Work through a strategy to adjust your anxiety levels.
3. Engage in some deep controlled breathing. Inhale as deeply as you can, hold the breath for a beat, then exhale slowly through the mouth.
4. Use an app like Calm or Relax Melodies to help you regulate your breath, meditate, or conduct a brief body scan
5. Aware, acknowledge, accept, amend
6. Work through some self-evaluation questions
7. Try a grounding exercise like the one shared at the end of this chapter
8. Once you have worked through your strategies, re-assess your SUD score, and document it.

Grounding Exercise

Whenever you feel like you are having an attack of sudden anxiety, you might feel as though you are not fully in your body. This sense of depersonalization can be quite disturbing and may lead to even more anxiety. Practice this simple grounding technique to help you remain connected to your physical space. Take a deep breath. Hold it for a few seconds. Slowly exhale through your mouth as though you were breathing through a straw. Look around the space that you're in.

What are five things that you can see? Lock eyes on those things. Catalog their features. Focus on them with intention.

What are four things you can touch? Touch each item. Note the temperature, texture, and other qualities of each thing.

What are three things you can hear? Notice the ticking of the clock. The whirring of the air cleaner. The drip, drip, drip of the kitchen sink. The fan on your laptop computer.

What are two things you can smell? Do you have essential oils in your space? Open a bottle and take a whiff. Are you stuck looking for something to smell? Check your armpits! You'll either notice the odor of your deodorant, or not...

What is one thing you can taste? Candy, gum, chocolate, even a glass of water will help you to regain your sense of space.

CHAPTER 15

Ouch! Responding to Hurtful words

"Sticks and stones may break my bones, but words will never hurt me."

Did your parents or teachers encourage you to recite this little poem when you were young? Did you use it as a response to other children on the playground when they were making fun of you? Did you find that even as you recited the words, they didn't quite numb the sting of pain you felt?

In my book, Bullying is Not a Game, Amanda's experience with bullying is shared. Her "friend group" turned on her at the urging of one frenemy within the group. They poked her with pins, beat her with belts on the playground, and they put fake blood in her locker because they knew that the sight of blood made her sick. Beyond that, they started rumours about her. They told her she was fat. Ugly. Her clothing choices were stupid. They started an online chat where people could post mean things about her. When she started getting sick from the anxiety and started missing school, they started a rumour that she was pregnant and that was why she was absent. Amanda had to drop out of school entirely, and as the bullying continued from elementary school to high school, she eventually chose to complete her education using an alternate schooling system.

Marnie* went through something very similar when her friend group turned on her. Using Snapchat and other online platforms, they spread lies about her, knowing that she could see the threads of demeaning conversations. They ignored her at school but showed up at places where she was going to be with the few friends she had left. They would call her names, make fun of her in public, and threaten to hurt her if they got her alone. She began refusing to go to school, and she was glued to her phone, watching to see if people were talking trash about her online.

I could share several other tales that reflect the same truth. Words have power. The truth is that relational bullying hurts more than physical bullying does. Bullying happens every seven minutes on the playground, and every 25 minutes in the classroom[1], and the most harmful form is relational or social bullying. This is when people say mean things, call names, ostracize former friends from a group, or point out their differences as a reason to be excluded. Relational bullying extends to cyberbullying, as 60% of youths say they like to interact online anonymously. 17% of those respondents admitted they preferred anonymity online because it allowed them to say mean things about other people and *get away with it.*[2] Yes. You heard that right.

The Truth about Relational Bullying

A study of teachers in training in the state of Arizona invited a group of student teachers to review a grouping of bullying scenarios. These teachers-in-training perceived relational bullying as the least harmful form of bullying, and they expressed the *least* empathy for victims of relational bullying[3]. Another study with school counsellors resulted in alarmingly similar findings. After reviewing scenarios involving physical, verbal, and relational bullying, the school counsellors perceived relational bullying as the least severe of the three forms of bullying. Furthermore, the counsellors expressed the least amount of empathy for children who were victims of relational bullying, and they were least likely to intervene in those types of incidents[4]. Conversely, counsellors who received bullying-specific training perceived relational bullying as more severe and expressed more empathy for victims of relational bullying[5].

Words Wound the Spirit

What does that tell us? Words have power. They hurt. The things you say about a person reflect what you think and feel about them. These words are often taken to heart and perceived by the recipient as a reflection of *who they are* rather than what you think of them. Why is it that people who have been maligned either publicly or privately feel hurt, anger, or shame even when the things that are reported about them are not true? They feel hurt because words have the innate ability to wound one's spirit. They feel anger because their expectations of friendship, loyalty, or kinship have been unmet, or perhaps angry because their rules about how friendship should operate have been violated, and trust has been betrayed. But they feel shame because people choose to believe the lies. Because that people could so easily believe those lies must mean that somehow you must be the horrible person that they described you to be. Shame creeps in when hurtful words succeed in making you feel bad about yourself.

The Tongue is Feral

The Bible tells us a few things about words. James chapter 3: 5-10 says this:

"the tongue is a little member and boasts great things. See how great a forest a little fire kindles! And the tongue *is* a fire, a world of iniquity. The tongue is so set among our members that it defiles the whole body., and sets on fire the course of nature; and it is set on fire by hell... *No man can tame the tongue.* It is an unruly evil, full of deadly poison. With it we bless our God and Father, and with it we curse *men, who have been made in the image of God* (emphasis mine). Out of the same mouth proceed blessing and cursing. My brethren, these things ought not to be so."

Wow! That's a pretty harsh statement about that thing we use to taste food and to form words! Did you notice that the passage clearly states that we can have the ability to bless, and that as easily as we can create beauty with our words, we are also capable of manifesting great destruction, just with the words we say! Remember that we are made in God's image, and while we might not have the power to create something out of nothing, our words do have a great measure of power.

Hebrews 4:12 says, "the word of God is quick (*alive*) and powerful, and sharper than any two-edged sword, piercing even to the dividing asunder of soul and spirit, and of the joints and marrow, and is a discerner of the thoughts of intents of the heart." His word can do that because He is an all-powerful, all-knowing God. But check this out: Proverbs 18:21 tells us that death and life are in the power of the tongue. This supports James's statement that the tongue can produce both blessing and cursing. Look at how Job begged his frenemies to just stop talking:

How long wilt thou speak these things? and how long shall the words of thy mouth be like a strong wind? (Job 8:2)

How long will it be ere ye make an end of words? (Job 18:2)

How long will ye vex my soul, and break me in pieces with words? (Job 19:2)

Our words have power.

Proverbs 6 shares seven things that God hates, and that list includes a lying tongue, a wicked heart, mischief-making, false witnesses (liars), and people who sow discord. Isn't it interesting that so many of the things God despises have to do with our words? BTW, don't get sidetracked by the "wicked heart" part, because we know that the words we speak come out of our hearts (Matthew 12:34 and Matthew 15:18). When people say hurtful things, those words cannot be unsaid. Sure, people can apologize, but the words stay with you, they stay in your brain, rattling around and searching for evidence of their truth. That's why they hurt. They call to mind every time you may have doubted yourself, or thought little of yourself, and the brain presents those memories to you as proof that what was said about you is true.

As this is a book on emotional mastery, let's explore how you can first protect yourself against hurtful words, harmful criticisms, and unfair or untrue reports about you. Second, I want to provide you with some strategies to help you control the unruliest member of your body, and to use your words in ways that bless, heal, and create harmony rather than destruction.

How to Insulate Yourself against Hurtful Words

1. **Acknowledge only what is true.** Often people will use inflammatory language as a way to incite anger, or to provoke an argument. Exaggerating the truth or fabricating nasty narratives is a great way to sidetrack you from the real issue or to put you on the defensive. Focus only on what is true and ignore the rest.

2. **What does this mean?** Remind yourself that nothing in life has any meaning except the meaning you give it. Say it again. Nothing has meaning except the meaning you give it. If you can determine that most of the things people say really mean nothing, or carry very little lifetime value, they will have no emotional hold over you.

3. **Fight words with words of your own.** By this I do not mean that you should come up with even meaner things to say, or to start your own smear

campaign on Snapchat or Instagram. Speak words of life over *yourself*! Speak your "IAM" statement over your life. Lies and unfair labels, accusations, or assumptions people make about you lose their power when you counter them with the truths of who God says you are. Remember, death *and* life; cursing *and* blessing are in the power of the tongue. You get to choose to speak blessings over yourself and others rather than allowing the harmful, hurtful words of others to settle over you like a shroud. Save the comebacks you'd like to shove in the face of your frenemies. Instead, speak life. Proverbs 15:1 says, "A soft answer turns away wrath, but grievous words stir up anger."

4. **Turn it around.** Jesus himself gave us instruction on how to deal with meanie-mouths. "Love your enemies, bless them that curse you, do good to them that hate you, and pray for them which despitefully use you and persecute you (Matt. 5:44). In the next section, I'll give you some strategies on how to do exactly that.

5. **Know God's got you.** In Genesis 12, there is added incentive for not getting caught up in the battle of words. God promises, "I will bless them that bless you, and curse them that curse you." You see, God's got you! You don't need to fight the way others do. We are encouraged not to seek revenge, and not to repay evil for evil, but to repay evil with good. Sounds crazy, doesn't it, especially when it is so easy to go online, cloak yourself in anonymity, and let the vitriol fly? The thing is, vengeance belongs to God, and He will fight your battles for you. Sure, you can take them up on your own, but why would you, when you have an all-powerful God at your back?

This last point brings me to strategies for keeping yourself from being the one with a sharp, hateful tongue.

Watch Your Mouth! How to Prevent Yourself from Harming Others with Your Words

1. **Test yourself.** Anytime you open your mouth to speak, run it through this test formulated by Bernard Meltzer:
2. Is it true?
3. Is it kind?
4. Is it necessary?
5. Is it helpful?

If the answer is no, you have two choices. You can say nothing at all. Sometimes silence really is golden. You can also choose to reframe your words until the answer to all four test questions is, "yes".

1. **Speak the truth in love.** Ephesians 4:15 encourages us to do this. My former pastor used to say, "Truth without love is a hammer; love without truth is hypocrisy." Whenever we need to speak, especially where there is conflict, we must balance the truths of our arguments with love and compassion. How can you do that?
2. **Get clarity.** Be very clear about the things you want to say before you open your mouth. One of the things I encourage my clients to do when they have a difficult conversation looming on the horizon, is to write down all their thoughts and feelings about the situation in question. This gives them an outlet for all the anger, hurt, fear, pain, shame, whatever – before they

confront the other party. Doing this allows for them to process some of the emotion and to make space in the upstairs brain for more rational thought. When the time comes for a face-to-face or even a written interaction, time and thoughtfulness coupled with clarity will ease the conversation along without you needing to resort to harsh words.

3. **Set your intentions and know your desired outcomes.** What do you want to see happen because of this communication? What are your long-term desired outcomes? Would you like to stay friends with the other party? Would you like your love interest to still be interested? Would you like to keep your job? Get along better with your parents? Have less conflict between members of your sports team? Have a better relationship with your siblings? Want the bullies to leave you alone?

Whatever your intention or your desired outcome, you should know exactly what you are going for when you engage the other party. Choose your words wisely, based on your long-term desires. Remember the thought matrix? It begins with your thoughts. Direct your thoughts towards your desired outcomes so that you can make more informed, thoughtful choices about how you will respond. Choosing your words carefully is easier when you have a desired end in mind *and* when you are filtering your angry or hurt thoughts through the questions noted earlier.

4. **Lastly, learn to set your ego aside.** Listen up, no matter what social media, television, advertisers, or popular culture would have you believe, it's not all about you. Nor does it have to be. When you set your ego aside, you stop REACTING and start RESPONDING. You will know your ego is engaged when you are in a position of defending yourself or saying things with the intent to WIN rather than RESOLVE an argument, or when you are

more concerned with feeling good about yourself than building a healthier relationship.

That old rhyme about sticks and stones is a lie. Words have power. More power than you can imagine. Life and death, blessings and curses are in the power of the tongue (Proverbs 18:21). You have power. Never forget that with great power also comes great responsibility! Choose and use your words wisely, and whenever it is in your power to do so, speak life.

CHAPTER 16

Depression and The Spirit of Heaviness

Dave was only seventeen years old when he was thrust into a job that brought with it fame, fortune, everything he could ever want. He was a conscientious, hard-working, good-looking young man. Easy on the eyes and easy to like. He thought his life was charmed until his boss, a jealous, insecure leader grew more and more resentful of Dave's popularity. Suddenly, Dave found himself experiencing the worst kind of bullying, so severe that he feared for his life. He fell into a deep state of depression and struggled with emotional regulation for years.

Constance* also found herself in a position where she was bullied at work so relentlessly that one day, without fully realizing what she was doing, she navigated her vehicle into a busy intersection, hoping that she would be hit and be fatally injured.

Randy* confessed that many times when driving over the Burlington Skyway bridge, he would hear a voice in his head saying, "You could just drive off the edge, and you would be out of your misery." The intrusive, suicidal thoughts distressed him even worse than his feelings of depression.

Depression has become a pandemic of its own, with an

increase in suicides among young Canadian women, a clear correlation between exposure to screen time and depression in youth aged 12-24, fear for the future, years of upheaval and an absence of structure or normalcy for secondary and post-secondary students, obsession with body image and plunging self-esteem only the tip of the iceberg.

Depression is No Laughing Matter

How often have you heard one of your peers exclaim, "Something happened and now I'm so depressed!"

"The hairdresser cut my hair wrong, and I'm so depressed."

"I only got a 69% on my test and I'm so depressed."

"I like that guy, but he doesn't like me – I'm so depressed."

Depression has become so commonplace that the reality of the disorder is often trivialized, and the *label* is used to express feelings of disappointment, discouragement, sadness, or contextual feelings of failure. Depression is none of these things! Depression is characterized by persistent feelings of low mood, aversion, or lack of motivation to engage in activity, sadness, and impulsivity. Some common characteristics of general depression include:

- Low mood
- Feelings of guilt, worthlessness, helplessness, or hopelessness
- Loss of interest or pleasure in activities that were once enjoyed
- Significant changes in weight or appetite
- Sleep disturbances (sleeping too much or too little)
- Decreased energy or fatigue (without significant physical exertion, or other organic reason)
- Thoughts of death or self-harm
- Poor concentration, focus, or attention, or difficulty making decisions

Depression looks and feels different for everyone. For some people like US President Abraham Lincoln or author, Virginia Wolf, clinical depression came with spending several weeks at a time closed off from the world in a room with the curtains drawn. Others can carry on with their lives, appearing to be coping if not entirely happy with the stressors they are facing. Others may find themselves somewhere in the in-between, forcing themselves to go to work or school each day, yet crying in private, experiencing losses in appetite and lack of motivation to connect with friends. Some people can function through their depression, managing to cope until their biochemistry balances on its own; others need medication to help properly balance the neurochemicals in their brain. There is no perfect answer since we are all unique and respond differently to treatments.

"You Just Need to Pray More"

A minister asked me how Christians could have mental illnesses like depression since when we come to Christ, the Holy Spirit makes us new, and we are transformed by the renewing of our minds[1]. He wondered if people just prayed more, and devoted themselves to the study of God's word, if this would be enough to heal one of depression. This thinking is rooted in the misconception that mental illness is a manifestation of demonic possession, and the idea that demonic spirits must flee from the presence of the Holy Spirit.

The thing is that the brain and the mind are not the same thing. Yes, we can be transformed by the renewing of our minds, but the mind is not a tangible, measurable, living, breathing organism like the brain is. The brain is the body's nerve center. It is the root of life: respiration, blood circulation, all our bodily functions, blinking, swallowing, gross and fine motor skills, sensation, and perception, all are controlled by the brain.

The brain is an organ, as is the heart, the liver, or the kidneys.

If all the body's organs can become diseased, it is not unreasonable to expect that the brain can also become diseased. What is Alzheimer's Disease or the various other forms of dementia, aneurisms, or strokes, if not disorders, diseases, or illnesses effecting the brain?

The Spirit of Heaviness

That is not to say that there isn't a spiritual component to depression. Depression manifests as a heaviness of the spirit. In fact, Isaiah 61:1-3 declares:

"The Spirit of the Lord GOD is upon me; because the LORD hath anointed me to preach good tidings unto the meek; he hath sent me to bind up the broken-hearted, to proclaim liberty to the captives, and the opening of the prison to them that are bound; to proclaim the acceptable year of the LORD, and the day of vengeance of our God; to comfort all that mourn; to appoint unto them that mourn in Zion, to give unto them beauty for ashes, the oil of joy for mourning, the garment of praise for the spirit of heaviness; that they might be called trees of righteousness, the planting of the LORD, that he might be glorified."

Much of this prophetic word speaks of broken hearts, people who are bound physically as well as spiritually, and those who are weighted down with a heavy spirit.

I can think of no better way to describe depression. In my youth and in periods throughout my adulthood, I have experienced bouts of depression, and it feels exactly like that. Heavy. Heavy limbs. Heavy heart. Heavy spirit. Heavy head. Heavy emotions. Depression is in actuality a dampening or a heaviness of the nervous system. It is, indeed, a heaviness of spirit, one that is referenced throughout the Bible:

"... I arose up from my heaviness" (Ezra 9:5)

"... I will leave off my heaviness, and comfort myself" (Job 9:27)

"Reproach hath broken my heart; and I am full of heaviness: and I looked for some to take pity, but there was none; and for comforters, but I found none." (Psalms 69:20)

"My soul melteth for heaviness: strengthen thou me according unto thy word." (Psalms 119:28)

I think of folks who experienced that heaviness of spirit in the Bible: Naomi – Ruth's mother-in-law encouraged people to call her Mara, meaning *bitter*. Jonah was impulsive, angry, and depressed. On impulse, he ran away, attempting to escape God's intention for his ministry. On the boat in the midst of the tempest, he impulsively told the sailors to throw him overboard. When God saved him and he eventually went to Joppa to do what he was supposed to do, he again grew angry and depressed when God preserved the repentant city instead of destroying it. Jonah even says, it would be better for him to die (Johan 4:3). Likewise, Elijah experienced one of the greatest miracles of his ministry when God answered his prayer for rain after three years of drought. However, when he was threatened by Queen Jezebel, he an off into hiding and fell into depression, saying like Jonah that it would be better for him to die (1 Kings 19:1-4).

Then, there is Dave, aka King David. He struggled with depression before and throughout his career as king over Israel. In the years that he was a fugitive running away from his boss, King Saul, and in the many years that followed, when his kingdom was almost overthrown by his son and his trusted advisors, David wrote many poems and songs describing his depressed state.

"How long wilt thou forget me, O LORD? for ever? how long wilt thou hide thy face from me?" (Psalms 13:1)

"How long shall I take counsel in my soul, having sorrow in my heart daily? how long shall mine enemy be exalted over me?" (Psalms 13:2)

"LORD, how long shall the wicked, how long shall the wicked triumph? How long shall they utter and speak hard things? and all the workers of iniquity boast themselves?" (Psalms 94:3-4)

You see, David understood depression. He felt forgotten, isolated, and downtrodden, and it wasn't just a passing sadness. He felt sorrow in his heart daily. He felt as though God had forgotten him forever. Yet, whenever he felt overcome by his feelings, he turned to the God of his salvation for comfort: "From the end of the earth will I cry unto thee, when my heart is overwhelmed: lead me to the rock that is higher than I." (Psalms 61:2)

God's Creation: The Beauty and Restorative Nature of... Nature

When I am working with depressed clients, I always begin with what I call the "low hanging fruit". Depression has organic origins, so why not begin by dealing with organic solutions? The beauty of God and His creation is that many of the solutions we need for our problems are right in front of us. Remember, the brain is organic matter, made up of 80% water. Two things the brain needs to remain functional are hydration and oxygenation. Here are some low-hanging fruit remedies for symptoms associated with persistent depression:

1. **Get outside**. Sunlight is a natural source of Vitamin D. Get outside, soak up the sun!
2. Breathe in the fresh air. While you are outside, practice breathing deeply and using the breathing technique shared in the chapter on anxiety.
3. **Get grounded.** Earthing or grounding is the practice of connecting your body with the earth's natural current. The easiest way to do this is to simply walk barefoot on grass, dirt, or sand. The benefits of earthing are many, and they have been empirically documented: "Reconnection with the Earth's electrons has been found to promote intriguing physiological changes and subjective reports of well-

being. Earthing (or grounding) refers to the discovery of benefits—including better sleep and reduced pain—from walking barefoot outside or sitting, working, or sleeping indoors connected to conductive systems that transfer the Earth's electrons from the ground into the body." (Source:

4. **Talk to another human – one who is trained as a therapist.** Never forget that God uses people to do His work. Seek out a therapist who is faith-informed, who can come alongside and support you as you learn how to live with bouts of depression. It is important to remember too, that depression can often be a partner to post-traumatic stress, or an after-effect of ACEs, making it even more important to have a good therapist to help you unpack the non-organic components of your symptoms.

5. **Be like Dave.** David's way was to repeatedly return to God with an attitude of praise and worship. No matter his circumstances, he sought the face of God, and always remembered to praise God regardless of the situation. This was the thing that helped him to function and thrive despite his depression, and it is this aspect of his character that earned him the title, "man after God's own heart."

What if you're still depressed?

You might find that your depression symptoms persist despite all these natural interventions. If this is true for you, it is advisable to speak about options for medication with a physician who is well-versed in mental health. Needing medication does not make you weak. It is not a reflection of your character, or your faith in God. Remember, the brain is an organ, and it is subject to illness just as is the rest of the body. If a person with diabetes requires insulin, and another with cancer requires chemotherapy, so a person with depression may require medication to help bring balance to the brain's neurochemistry. Do not be afraid or ashamed to research this option as another intervention to complement the natural solutions shared above. The need for medication may only be a temporary solution until therapy has helped you to resolve the underlying reasons for the depression; or, it may be something that is required over the long-term to help your brain chemistry remain balanced.

CHAPTER 17

Guilt and Shame

Janice* cringed and winced, bracing herself for her parents' reaction to her new tattoo. She had it done without their knowledge despite knowing they disapproved of body art. She reasoned, "I'm eighteen now. I'm an adult, I can make my own choices." It was her body, and she wanted a tattoo. Even so, she dreaded hearing the words, "We're so disappointed in you."

Soraya's* boyfriend decided they needed time apart. Her mental health had been unstable for a while, and he felt emotionally overwhelmed, crumbling under the weight of compassion fatigue. "I feel worthless," she cried. "It's like my problems were too much for him. I was too much for him. I'm worthless and unattractive. No one will want to be with a person like me."

Jennifer* held back tears as she mused, "I can never seem to get to the point of asking 'what did I do wrong?' I always default to the assumption that there is something wrong with me."

Guilt and shame are as inevitable experiences as death and taxes. From the time we are toddlers testing out our parents' boundaries all the way to our death beds, we are prone to experience bouts of guilt and feelings of shame.

Here's the difference between the two: guilt is feeling remorse or regret for something you did, or for something you failed to do. For example, Janice got a tattoo against her parents' wishes. She might feel remorseful for a perceived disrespect of their values. That is guilt.

Shame is a feeling associated with the way you or others perceive you as a person. Shame is a deep sense of embarrassment that is based on who you are – your character – as opposed to something you did or did not do.

Shame compounds guilt. Soraya felt remorse for not having addressed her declining mental health sooner. That's guilt. That shame compounded her guilt is evidenced by her feeling like there was something wrong with her. Jennifer expressed it most clearly when she identified the *guilt* question – *what did she do wrong?* This question was overshadowed by the *shame* question, *'what's wrong with me?'*

You are More Than the Sum of Your Deeds

What we hear when our parents say, "We're so disappointed in you" is "You should be ashamed of yourself." As a parent, I want to challenge those statements and the interpretations that accompany them. What parents really mean is they are disappointed in your *choices* and actions, not *you* as a person.

Here's the thing. Parents have a mandate to train up their children in the way they should go (Proverbs 23:6), to discipline them, and to teach them wisdom (Proverbs 23: 15-16) so that they can grow up to be responsible, contributing members of society. Christian parents are further tasked with raising their children in the fear (respect) of God and teaching them to live by Godly principles. The thing is that parents only know what they know. They often end up parroting the language they heard growing up, repeating the same disciplinary actions that their parents did, and making the same parenting mistakes. Even though the words they use may hurt, they may not have learned how to do or say things any different or any better. Unfortunately, kids don't come with a user manual, and parents often find themselves struggling with finding the right way to communicate displeasure or discipline to their children.

Are we simply the sum of our deeds or are we more than that? Should we be ashamed for who we are? Must we carry the guilt and remorse for past deeds with us for our entire lives?

No Condemnation

Romans 8:1 tells us that *"There is therefore now no condemnation to them which are in Christ Jesus, who walk not after the flesh, but after the Spirit."* John 3:16-19 tells us that God loved us so much that He sacrificed His only son so that those of us who believe in him (those who are in Christ Jesus) would not perish but have everlasting life. John goes on to say that condemnation lies in knowing the source of light but choosing to continue to walk in darkness. Look, this doesn't mean that you are expected to be perfect. When you choose to walk in light, you may make mistakes – we all do – but you are covered in grace. A repentant heart (a broken and a contrite heart) will not be despised or rejected by God[1]. The word further tells us that Jesus bore our shame to the cross so that we would not have to carry that burden.[2]

When Your Heart is Overwhelmed

Battling feelings of overwhelming guilt and shame can be a real challenge. Even after we have repented for our wrongdoing, and have taken appropriate steps to make amends, sometimes the guilt we feel for what we did or did not do becomes a burden we carry around with us for years. It is hard to believe that anyone else would offer us forgiveness, let alone the God of the universe when we have such difficulty forgiving ourselves. It's even worse when the people whose opinions we value the most cause us to feel as though our mistakes are unforgivable, because that compounds our guilt with feelings of deep shame.

Whenever I think of guilt from the perspective of my faith, I always turn to Psalm 51. This heartfelt cry of repentance from David after his colossal mess-up with Bathsheba and the murder of her husband, Uriah, reminds me of how great a mistake we can make and still find grace in the eyes of God.

Psalms 51:1 To the chief Musician, A Psalm of David, when Nathan the prophet came unto him, after he had gone in to Bathsheba. Have mercy upon me, O God, according to thy lovingkindness: according unto the multitude of thy tender mercies blot out my transgressions. Wash me throughly from mine iniquity, and cleanse me from my sin. For I acknowledge my transgressions: and my sin is ever before me. Against thee, thee only, have I sinned, and done this evil in thy sight: that thou mightest be justified when thou speakest, and be clear when thou judgest. behold, I was shapen in iniquity; and in sin did my mother conceive me. Behold, thou desirest truth in the inward parts: and in the hidden part thou shalt make me to know wisdom. Purge me with hyssop, and I shall be clean: wash me, and I shall be whiter than snow. Make me to hear joy and gladness; that the bones which thou hast broken may rejoice. Hide thy face from my sins, and blot out all mine iniquities. Create in me a clean heart, O God; and renew a right spirit within me. Cast me not away from thy presence; and take not thy holy spirit from me. Restore unto me the joy of thy salvation; and uphold me with thy free spirit. Then will I teach transgressors thy ways; and sinners shall be converted unto thee. Deliver me from bloodguiltiness, O God, thou God of my salvation: and my tongue shall sing aloud of thy righteousness. O Lord, open thou my lips; and my mouth shall shew forth thy praise. For thou desirest not sacrifice; else would I give it: thou delightest not in burnt offering. The sacrifices of God are a broken spirit: a broken and a contrite heart, O God, thou wilt not despise. Do good in thy good pleasure unto Zion: build thou the walls of Jerusalem. Then shalt thou be pleased with the sacrifices of right-

eousness, with burnt offering and whole burnt offering: then shall they offer bullocks upon thine altar.

David acknowledged his mistake. He made it clear that despite his actions harming a whole bunch of people, his greatest offense was in his disrespect of God's commandments. His remorse was sincere, and he acknowledged what God would most respect in terms of an attempt at restitution. "Thou desirest not sacrifice; else would I give it: thou delightest not in burn offering. The sacrifices of God are a broken spirit: a broken and a contrite heart, O God, thou wilt not despise." The most important thing is that David accepted the consequences of his actions, and he resolved to never make the same mistake again.

We can do the same. We can make a heartfelt prayer of repentance to God for the things we are guilty of and commit to making restitution to those we have harmed. We can turn away from our misdeeds and be resolute in our commitment to not make the same mistakes again.

Overcoming shame comes back around to loving and accepting yourself and who you are in Christ. I mean, if God loves and accepts you, surely you can find a little grace for yourself! Look back on the concepts you learned in chapter ## when you did the research into who and Whose you are (You did do that homework, didn't you?). Neil Anderson of Freedom in Christ Ministries shares a list of scriptures that he uses to remind himself that he is accepted, secure, and significant to God. I'm sharing some of his favourites here along with my own, in the hopes that they will bring you some comfort and reassurance that you do not have to live in shame.

1. **I am known!** Psalm 139:1-3
2. **I am understood!** Psalm 139:4
3. **I am protected!** Psalm 139:5, Psalm 32:7-8
4. **I am surrounded. I am never alone!** Psalm 139: 6-12

5. **I am God's child!** Psalm 139: 13-14, Psalm 27:10, Romans 8:15, Galatians 4:5, Ephesians 1:5, John 1:2, Ephesians 2:18

6. **I am accepted!** John 15:15, 1 Corinthians 6:17, 19-20, Colossians 2:10, Psalm 139:15-16.

7. **I am precious, I am valued, and I am loved!** Psalm 139:17-18, John 3:16, Romans 8:35, Philippians 1:6, 2 Timothy 1:7, 1 John 5:18, 1 Peter 5:7, Deuteronomy 32:10, Jeremiah 31:3

8. **I am strong!** Isaiah 40:31, Isaiah 41:10, Philippians 4:13

9. **I am forgiven and free!** I do not have to walk in shame! Romans 5:1, Romans 8:31, Philippians 3:20, 1 John 5:18, 1 John 1:9, John 8:36, Colossians 1:14

10. **I have a purpose!** Jeremiah 29:11, 1 Peter 2:9, Romans 8:28, Philippians 1:6

Whenever you feel overwhelmed by shame, remind yourself that *feelings lie*. Remember what the wisest man who ever lived said: trust in God with your whole heart – do not rely on your feelings.[3] You are not your deeds, nor are you what you *feel* you are. Get your identity securely rooted and grounded in Christ and who God says you are. Say goodbye to guilt by making things right in your heart and by reconciling with those you harmed. Shrug off the heavy blanket of shame, knowing that God doesn't see you that way. He has covered you in His mercy and grace.

CHAPTER 18

The Truth about Relationships

We had been friends for ten years. I trusted her like a sister; our families spent time together over Christmas holidays as a tradition. I stood by her while she went through some seriously dark times, and she had done the same for me. I thought we would be BFFs for life. Then suddenly, over the course of about two weeks, the whole thing began to disintegrate until what seemed a solid friendship imploded on itself, and we were done.

I'm not gonna lie, it took me several weeks to recover from the gut-wrenching pain of that loss. We had been such a key part of each other's lives. Then just like that, it was over. Had I paid attention, I might have noticed red flags popping up. But I was too invested in the friendship and lacked the self-confidence to do anything about the warning signs that the relationship was becoming toxic.

I noticed several boundary violations, but I ignored them. I reasoned away the unacceptable behaviour because she was my friend. I said nothing when she did things that were hurtful. By the time I had enough and was ready to reinforce my boundaries, it was too late. I had taught her how to treat me, and she was not interested in learning to do things differently.

I cried for days. Pleaded with her to talk things through with me so that we could re-define our friendship. Her response was that she was moving forward with the mindset that she once had a good friend, but that she had died. In other words, I was dead to her.

The truth is that some people come into your life for a reason, some for a season, and others for a lifetime. When those "reasons" no longer exist, and those "seasons" change, it hurts. A lot. Platonic friendships break up too, and the pain and heartache are as real as any other loss.

Fences Make Good Neighbours: The Value of Healthy Boundaries

There are different types of boundaries. **Physical boundaries** are in reference to personal space and physical touch. If someone touches you or remains in your personal space when you don't want them to, that would be a physical boundary violation. For example, approaching a pregnant woman and touching her swollen tummy without asking for permission is a boundary violation. Intellectual boundaries are about thoughts and ideas. Dismissing someone's ideas or belittling them is an example of an intellectual boundary violation. **Emotional boundaries** are all about feelings. A way to express an emotional boundary might be choosing when, where, and how much personal information you share. A violation of an emotional boundary would be minimizing someone's feelings or discounting their emotional state.

Sexual boundaries are about the emotional, intellectual, and physical aspects of sexuality. Mutual understanding and respect of limitations around sex is healthy (including wanting to wait until marriage). Sexual boundary violations include unwanted sexual touching, pressure to engage in sexual behaviours, leering, or sexual comments. **Material boundaries** are about the things you own or your finances. You get to choose how and with whom you share your material possessions. A material boundary violation might be someone borrowing something of yours and not returning it, pressuring you to give or loan things out, or stealing your money or possessions. **Time boundaries** refer to how you use your time. You need to be able to budget your time, and you have the right to set limits about how much time you give to work, relationship, hobbies, or community. A time violation might look like making too many demands on a person's time.[1]

I didn't notice the many boundary violations that had been occurring over the years in my friendship. Emotional boundary violations, material boundary violations, time boundary violations, even intellectual boundary violations. Part of why I was loathe to call out the several violations of my boundaries was my own insecurity. I placed more value on the friendship than I did my own personal needs.

It Begins with You

William Glasser says that every problem is, at its heart, a relationship problem. The foundation of all relationships that will determine if they stand the test of time or fail, is communication. How do you talk to yourself? The things you say to yourself matter. Remember that words have power. One of the through-lines of this book has been the notion of knowing who you are and Whose you are. If you do not love and accept yourself, the *you* that God made you to be, the *you* that He created with and for a purpose, the *you* that He so loved that He gave His only Son for you, you will carry that insecurity and self-loathing into every relationship you have. If you can't trust your own judgement and you have difficulty trusting God's plan for you, you will reflect that mistrust in your human relationships.

To cultivate healthy relationships with others, you've got to start by nurturing your relationship with yourself.

1. Know Whose you are (see chapter 5 on ACEs)
2. Know who you are (see chapter 6 on Self-Esteem)
3. Understand and assert your boundaries. When people violate your boundaries, let them know. You can do that respectfully and compassionately, speaking the truth in love (Ephesians 4:15).
4. When someone you care about says or does something hurtful, take some time to process the hurt using TSA.

Let's do a quick recap of TSA:

- **THINK**: What is happening? What does it mean? How do I feel about it? What is my desired outcome? What can I do to obtain that outcome without causing myself any long-term pain? What action will I settle on? What is the lifetime value of this event?
- **SAY**: Sometimes you need extra time and a little extra help to work through the right words to say. One of the tools I have used over the years to do this is letter writing. Letter writing is my go-to method of communication if the lifetime value of an event is significantly high. It allows me to process my thoughts, to read and re-ad my words and to edit them deeply before ever sharing my thoughts with anyone else. Here's the thing. I'm good with words. And when I feel deeply hurt or I am filled with rage (yes, it happens), I could do serious damage with my tongue. Now, I am aware that death and life, blessing and cursing are in the power of the tongue, and I do not want to speak death or cursing into anyone's life. Don't need that on my conscience. So, one of my personal boundaries is to shut my pie hole when my

frustration signal is activated. I hold that boundary as much for myself as I do for others. This is a non-negotiable for me.

- **ASK**: Engage the other party in a dialogue where possible and appropriate. Ask, "How can we work together to ensure this doesn't happen again?" Be ready to listen and collaborate as you negotiate a way forward together.

You can write a letter to help you process your thoughts using this template I borrowed from Jack Canfield's Self Esteem and Peak Performance, with a little add-on I learned from Lisa Nichols.

- Hurt
- Anger
- Fear
- Sorry for...
- I forgive you for...
- Thank you for giving me...

Here's an example based on the demise of my ten-year friendship.

Dear Jane,*

*I felt **hurt** when you implied that I was only your friend for selfish reasons. I was **angry** because the way you spun our argument was unfair, and the things you said are not true. I'm also angry that you just kept talking over me and you refused to listen to my side. I am **afraid** that our friendship might never recover from this – at the very least, it won't ever be like it was. I'm sorry for not being clearer on my boundaries sooner. That is on me. I'm also **sorry** for not being clearer in my communication with you, and that I wasn't better at showing you how important your friendship is to me. Please forgive me for that. I **forgive** you too, for the things in our friendship that frustrated me that I recognize were boundary violations. I* *forgive you for the hurtful words you said. Thank you for giving me the chance to recognize my mistakes in our friendship, and to realize that I need to be true to myself and my non-negotiables. Moving forward, I'd like us to think about what we want from our friendship. Perhaps, when we have both had time to reflect and calm down, we'll be able to talk about where we go from here. What I do know is that I'd like to remain friends, but we need to re-negotiate the terms of our friendship.*

The hallmarks of healthy relationships are assertive communication, healthy boundaries, forgiveness/acceptance, and intimacy. Consider these questions when evaluating your relationships. Do you like each other? Do you trust each other? Do you share common interests? Do you enjoy spending time together? Are you supportive of each other? Can you celebrate each other's wins? Can you be patient with each other? Can you be accepting of each other's differences? Are you able to set clear boundaries and are they respected? 1 Corinthians 13 speaks of the characteristics of love, and they apply even for platonic relationships. "Love is patient, kind, not envious, proud, or arrogant. Love does not behave unseemly; it is not selfish or easily provoked. Love doesn't think evil thoughts, nor does it rejoice in iniquity; rather, it rejoices in the truth."

Define Your Non-Negotiables

One last thing. I'd like to share a tool with you to help you get clear about your boundaries so you can cultivate healthy relationships. You are surrounded by people, places and things, all bombarding you with requests, needs, ideas, and problems. They are competing for whatever energy you have available, and they won't take no for an answer. At least they won't until you learn how to educate them on who you are, what they can, and can't do. Then your universe will begin to respect you and your needs.

. . .

How to Begin Educating Your Environment[2]

1. Start with defining your non-negotiables
2. What are your key values?
3. What is most important to you in your life? (Things, memories, your emotional state, whatever)
4. Who is most important to you in your life?
5. Ask yourself some key questions
6. If I had to choose between __________ and my values, what is more important?
7. Is my relationship with the most important people in my life worth risking for ____________________?
8. If I compromise my values to get what I want in the short term, how will I feel over time?
9. Will I still respect myself if I choose to do something that is outside the boundaries of my values?
10. Decide these things:
11. What is acceptable to you in terms of your own behaviour.
12. What is acceptable to you in terms of other people's behaviour.
13. What is not acceptable for you or for others.
14. What you need from other people.
15. Use proper phrasing to express your non-negotiables to others.
16. Share with others when they are doing or saying something that you don't appreciate.
17. Let people know what you want, need, or won't permit.
18. Remember you have the right to set your boundaries – tell others what they can and cannot say or do to – or with you.

19. Let people know what they can expect of you – the things you will not say or do because it interferes with your non-negotiables.
20. Try to keep yourself "Inventory-Free". This means that you aim to leave every encounter with nothing unsaid, nothing stepped over, nothing un-requested, and nothing not acknowledged or appreciated. You say what there is to say immediately when you sense it. This is important because:
21. What is left unsaid gets in the way of a relationship.
22. What is left unasked for is a missed opportunity.
23. When too much is left unsaid, "corrosion" results.

I had a boss who always yelled at the staff, "You teach people how to treat you!" The day he decided to call us all "bottom feeders" because all we did was focus on the poop in life, I realized he was right. We had been teaching him how to treat us, and I decided it was time for a new lesson. Drawing from my defined non-negotiables, I set out to correct him as gently as I could in the moment (because you have to know I was ripping mad) about why it was inappropriate to talk to his team that way. He ended up putting me in charge of developing standards for professional conduct in the workplace.

I know from experience what happens when bottling up our pain results in too many words unspoken and too many hurts unchallenged. Hearts get broken, trust is irrevocably damaged, and bitterness and resentment grow, choking out love. No matter the circumstance, you must find the strength, the confidence, and the self-esteem that is necessary to educate those around you about what is permissible in your life. Let me clear – the learning *must* begin and end with you. You must first unlearn destructive habits, re-frame your interpretations of events through self-evaluation, and decide what *you* will allow to produce stress, anger, and fear, or peace, joy, and passion in your life.

CHAPTER 19

Taking Response-Ability for Your Big Feelings

There once were two men named Jude and Pete. They were both friends to Jesus. They both followed Him. Both men had unique responsibilities within the group known as "the twelve disciples". And both men betrayed Jesus. Both were guilty of betraying a friend. Both felt shame. That's where the comparison ends. They had two very different outcomes.

You see, Pete truly loved Jesus and believed him to be the Messiah, the Son of God. Jude had some doubts; he was unsure if the last three years of his life following Jesus had been worth it. Pete was impulsive. And he often would just run to Jesus with whatever was bothering him like, "Hey, what about this? Why do I have to forgive my brother, and how many times do I have to do that?" On the other hand, Jude never said much. He hovered in the background. He was quiet.

Jude was also kind of selfish. We know that because the only time Judas ever spoke up was the time that Mary Magdalene came and broke open an alabaster box full of scented oils. The thing was *expensive*. It had *value*. She probably took the bulk of her savings to purchase that thing. And she didn't just pour the ointment out.

She *broke* the box! She broke it open and poured the oils on Jesus. That's when Judas spoke up saying, "Hey, she could have donated that to the cause, and we could have sold that for a lot of money."

Jude was the one who held the purse. He was like the ancient equivalent of the church secretary/treasurer. He was responsible for the money. You and I know that sometimes when people are responsible for the money, they stop seeing everything else and only see dollar signs. When you couple Jude's greed with his doubts, they fueled his intention for betraying Jesus. Jude went into his play to betray Jesus having fully engaged the decision-making power of his upstairs brain. Jude did what he did with *intention*. It wasn't an impulse; he thought it through. He went to the religious leaders in the temple, and he cut a bargain with them that he would deliver Jesus to them for a certain sum of money. His betrayal of Christ was *all the way* premeditated.

Pete's intentions for betraying Jesus were much simpler and much more visceral. He was *scared*. That's it. Peter was scared. He was terrified of being hunted, captured, tried, and crucified, and his down downstairs brain was speaking for him. His downstairs brain said, "Dude, if you get caught, you're gonna go out like they're gonna take Jesus out." He was afraid and he did what he did in an impulsive act of self-preservation.

Now, here is the interesting thing about how Jesus responded. Jesus's response was compassion for both men. See, God understands all the different aspects of our nature and, and he loves us just the same. He understood that Peter was afraid and that his downstairs brain was what responded to that fear.

Jesus also understood that Judas wasn't sure that the last three years of his life had been spent doing what he was supposed to do. He wasn't secure in his purpose as a disciple of Christ. So, when Jesus was in the garden, and Judas showed up with the religious leaders and soldiers, Jesus called to him, "Friend, fancy seeing you here!" Jesus didn't come at him with anger, or recrimination or accusations. He just said, "Hey, friend, what are you doing here?"[1]

I believe it was that the compassion that Jesus showed, the understanding that he offered, that determined how both men responded in kind. Peter wept bitterly and repented for what he had done. Because he had started out with a heart full of doubt and fueled by greed, Judas felt that he couldn't be forgiven. You see, Peter had had that conversation with Jesus about forgiving your brother seventy times seven, and he paid attention. Where was Judas during that conversation? He might have been there. He might not have been there. But if he was in the room, he wasn't listening, because he didn't hear Jesus say that if we don't forgive people who hurt us, neither will He forgive us.

Maybe Judas was listening, and perhaps that's part of why he did end up making the choice that he did - because he had unforgiveness in his heart towards other people. For whatever reason, Judas didn't feel like he could be forgiven. He went back and he tried to repent but he tried to repent to men, instead of repenting to God. He went back to the to the religious leaders and said, "I made a mistake. I shouldn't have done this. I don't want this money." And they replied, "We don't care. We got what we wanted. Whatever you do now is up to you."

They washed their hands of him. At that point, he didn't feel like he could go to God. There's a lesson in that! That tells me that just because we spend time with Jesus, just because we spend time in his presence, it doesn't necessarily mean that we are His. Spending time with him is not enough. We need to get to know Him. We need to have *relationship* with Him. We need to trust him.

Level up!

Think of *leveling up* like I talked about in chapter one. It's not enough to just believe that God *is*, and it's not enough to have an obscure, vague kind of faith. "Oh, yeah, I know. There's a God, and I know He cares about me." That's great, but to really trust Him – that's another level.

Had Judas really trusted Jesus, he would have heard the words spoken over him in the garden. He would have heard the compassion in those words. He would have watched and paid attention as Jesus healed the soldier whose ear Peter cut off. He would have heard Jesus when he was being crucified saying, "Father, forgive them. They don't know what they're doing."

Judas didn't pay attention to any of those things. He was so distraught, so caught up in his own depression, so covered in guilt and shame that he felt his only option was to take his own life. There's a lesson there too, several lessons in fact!

You have choices!

You can choose to level up your trust, to place your trust firmly in God to believe the things that he says about you. Remember Whose you are! Even when you make colossal mistakes, like both Peter and Judas did, you can step back and say, "You know what, I know God still loves me. If I turn to him now, He will not forsake me." That's the kind of leveled up trust you need to have.

You could walk away. You could choose to believe that you can't be forgiven. You could, like Judas, believe there's no coming back from your mistake. You have the choice to believe those things. But you don't have to, you can choose to believe what God says about Himself, and who you are in Him.

This is where the taking responsibility is important because you get to choose how you respond in any given situation. When you are on the receiving end of hurt, betrayal, or rejection, you can choose to respond as Jesus did with compassion, with understanding, with grace, and with forgiveness. Or you can choose to respond in anger. You can choose violence. You can choose to fight, you can choose to run, or you can choose to be a people pleaser and fawn. Any choice you make is going to have a corresponding outcome. You have choices; choose wisely.

Freedom in Forgiveness

Another valuable lesson that we can take from this is the power of forgiveness. Judas felt he was unforgivable, and he took his own life before he could learn any different. I mean, Judas had the nerve to accompany the guards into the Garden of Gethsemane to show them where Jesus was. Still, Jesus' response when He saw Judas approaching with the enemy was, "Friend, why have you come here?"

If anyone had reason to feel angry, hurt betrayed, and rejected, Jesus did, but He still chose to call Judas his friend. This was the last recorded "conversation" between Jesus and Judas, and I am sure that Jesus wanted Judas to know that He bore him no ill will. Jesus could have ranted and raved at Judas, which was entirely within His rights; however, He would have solidly reinforced Judas' belief that he was unforgivable. Rather, He wanted to be sure that Judas' memories of Jesus were of One who loved him despite his behaviours, his feelings, or his choices.

How Jesus forgives is a model for how He expects us to forgive. He gave us the guidelines in "the Lord's prayer" when He instructed us to pray, "forgive us our trespasses as we forgive those who trespass against us." He also made it clear that if we choose not to forgive, but to hold on to anger and resentment, then we should not expect to be forgiven of God[2]. These are tough words, but ones we must take to heart. If we wish to receive forgiveness from our Heavenly Father, we must find a way to forgive.

Peter, on the other hand, repented and sought forgiveness. When Jesus was resurrected and came to Peter, showing him the forgiveness, love and compassion that he craved, Peter accepted it. He could have rejected it and said, "You know what? I'm not deserving." But he accepted it.

When Jesus asked him later, "Peter, do you love me?" Peter told him the truth. "I do. I really do love you." He accepted the forgiveness and the love that was offered to him.

Your Mistakes Do Not Trump Your God-given Purpose

That brings us to our third lesson. Think about this. When Peter accepted the grace Jesus was offering, Jesus also awarded Peter responsibility. He gave this task to Peter, "You know what, I need you to take care of these people. I need you to feed my sheep, feed my lambs."

Don't forget, Peter had already been given a mandate. Peter knew his purpose. His purpose was to be the rock upon which the church would be founded[3]. He had been given that purpose before he messed up. It was because he understood the beauty of forgiveness that he was able to receive his own. He paid attention to the lessons that Jesus had taught them, and he was able to come back from that failure to be the person to preach the first sermon of the Christian church.

The giving and receiving of forgiveness are integral components of stepping into your purpose. Remember how Joe remained mindful of his purpose no matter what, and when the time came, he forgave his brothers in fulfillment of that purpose. Be like Joe.

E+R=O

There's an equation I learned from Jack Canfield, and I teach it to everyone whenever I have the opportunity. The equation simply says, Event plus Response equals Outcome. E+R=O.

That's it. Think back to what you learned in the introduction to Anger. An event occurs and you interpret it, decide if your expectations have been met, and assign meaning to that event. You then react or respond, and that reaction or response is followed by a consequence. Event plus Response equals Outcome. You learned some strategies for processing each event (T.S.A.) to help you properly evaluate each situation and to choose an intentional response that will hopefully get you to (or closer to) your desired outcome.

This chapter is titled "Taking Response-Ability" because I want to take you deeper into evaluating your responses. To that end, I want to share some self-evaluation questions to help you determine what belongs to you when it comes to your emotions and responsibility for your actions. Once you determine that, it's time to lay everything else (blame, guilt, and shame) that other people try to put on you.

Taking Response-ability

In every interaction with people in our lives, choosing a careful response is essential for healthy relationships. Think about the thought matrix and the choice matrix: you can make the right choice at the wrong time for the wrong reasons. You can make the wrong choice at the wrong time for the wrong reasons. You can make the wrong choice at the right time for the right reasons. You've got all kinds of options. What's important is that you continue to focus on your *desired outcome.*

Your desired outcome.

Your desired outcome.

Say that again, your desired outcome.

You need to focus on your desired outcome, not just the reaction that will make you feel better in this moment. Concentrate on the response that will help you to feel better *and* get you the best possible outcome over the long term.

It is so important to remember the importance of communication. Remember I said that Judas didn't say much, he really didn't have much to say at all, except for when it came to money. It appeared too that he wasn't listening all that much either. Peter was constantly asking questions, constantly getting into tricky situations, constantly shooting off his mouth. But he learned more, and what he learned came through for him when his life was in a crunch.

Likewise, when you are carefully evaluating each situation that you find yourself in, and you are tempted to take blame that isn't yours for whatever reason, keeping the peace, avoiding a confrontation, or just because your shoulders are broad enough to carry it, consider the long-term pain of taking on and carrying what was never yours to shoulder.

Consider the breakup of my ten-year platonic friendship as a case in point. Here is a summary of the process I went through to help me heal from the pain of the breakup.

Who said what? *She made several accusations and many of them were false. She said she would just pretend I had died, or basically that I was dead to her. I said I wanted to stay friends, but we needed to redefine the parameters of the friendship. I did not say anything hurtful or accusatory. I have nothing to feel remorseful about when it comes to my words.*

Who did what? *I can recall the things she did following the argument, and the efforts I made to reach out and reconcile. I have no regrets about my behaviour choices.*

What of this is mine to own? *I allowed the argument to go on for too long, as I tried to make sense of what she was blaming me for and trying to defend myself. I ignored the red flags in the friendship instead of addressing them. I did not respect myself enough to hold my boundary lines or to ask for what I needed in the friendship. I taught her how to treat me.*

What other aspects of this problem can I honestly say I hold no responsibility for? *I hold no responsibility for her expectations. I hold no responsibility for her choices. I hold no responsibility for the way she decided to express her emotions to me. Those things are not mine, and I will not carry them.*

Once I realized that I bore very little blame for the way things worked out (other than not respecting myself or my boundaries enough), letting go of the painful breakup was much easier. I knew my conscience was clear before God, and eventually I was able to move on from the relationship.

What If I Do Own Some Responsibility?

For the stuff we do own – repentance is key. We can ask for forgiveness from God and from the humans we have harmed. We can make reparations where possible. If you stole something, pay it back. If you damaged property, volunteer your time to repair it. If you wrote something hurtful anonymously on someone's social media, apologize and take the offending post down. You can do it!

It is also important to forgive yourself! Give yourself permission to make mistakes, to atone for them, and to receive the forgiveness of others, of God, and of yourself. If Dave could do it, so can you. Be like Dave.

One Final Story

E+R=O. Event + Response = Outcome. Several years ago, Evan* was vacationing with friends, and they decided to go spelunking or cave diving. Now, this is an activity that is not for the weak-minded or the claustrophobic. Evan and his friends were in full scuba gear, under water (of course) *and* under ground. Imagine swimming in the dark, surrounded by water and rock. The four men were navigating a tunnel and Evan was bringing up the rear. Evan is a tall guy, with broad shoulders and a bit of bulk. As he was maneuvering through the tunnel, he got stuck on a stalactite that impeded his movement.

Imagine this is you and think what this must have felt like in that moment. It is cold and dark. Your friends have gone ahead, and they have no idea that you have been left behind or that there is any kind of trouble. You're stuck in a tight space with limited mobility of your arms, and on top of that, you are underwater.

You have no method of communication, and a limited supply of air. What would you do?

Finding himself trapped in this literal hole, Evan realized that he had three options:

1. Panic – and die
2. Do nothing – and die
3. Calm down, find a way to get free, and live.

Which option do you think Evan chose? When the panic died down and he had evaluated the situation more rationally, he was able to focus on the problem at hand. If he had become stuck a certain way, then by undoing that motion, he could get unstuck. That is exactly what he did. Using small, controlled, subtle movements, he was able to free his gear from the obstruction, and by changing his positioning as carefully as he could, he was able to clear the tunnel – living to tell the tale.

What do you do when faced with stressful situations? Do you panic? Do you shut down? Do you go into fight mode? Do you seek to people please? Any of these responses will result in death – perhaps not the literal kind, but the death of the dream, goal, objective, or purpose that you were pursuing up until the point of crisis.

There is an inherent lesson in Evan's story. The *event* was that he found himself stuck. This was his crisis point. If events alone determined our outcomes, I wouldn't be telling you his story today. Evan would have died in that cave, and I never would have met him. What determined his outcome was his response. It is important to note too, that he could not change anything about the event itself. He could not somehow magically drain the water out of the cave. He could not move the rock wall to make the space wider for him to get through. The only thing he could change, or control was *himself*.

This is true for you as well. When you are faced with any kind of crisis (financial, mental, physical, or relational) your response will decide how things work out for you. If you allow your downstairs brain to take over whenever you are challenged – your outcome will be very different than if you express your feelings and needs appropriately, and rationally seek solutions to your problems. When you find yourself "stuck" in an impossible situation, remember you have three options. Panic, do nothing, OR master those big feelings, find a way to get free, and live.

About Julie Christiansen

Julie Christiansen has worked in church ministry since the age of eight when she joined a singing group dubbed, "The Sunshine Girls". In her teens, Julie participated in various choirs and singing groups, and took on roles within the Sunday School, Music, and Youth departments of her home church in Ottawa. After moving to Niagara, Julie and her husband worked as Youth Directors for seven years, and then another seven years as Music Directors before "retiring" from music ministry. At the time of publication, Julie continues to work in outreach, music, and pulpit ministries in support of grassroots evangelistic works.

Branded as "Oprah for the Office" and "The Anger Lady" by her clients, Julie has been compared to the likes of Brian Tracy and Jack Canfield. An internationally recognized speaker, and published author, Julie brings close to three decades experience in group and individual counselling. She holds a B.A. in Psychology and a M.A. in Counselling Psychology. Over the course of her career in academia, she taught courses at Brock University, TAPE Educational Services, Niagara College, and she served as adjunct professor at George Brown College for seven years. She is the principal of a thriving private psychotherapy practice serving residents across the province of Ontario.

Julie created the Anger Solutions™ Program, which has been delivered to both secular and faith-based organizations throughout Ontario. Anger Solutions has expanded beyond Ontario's borders and is now in use in several cities across Canada and internationally. As an expert on anger and stress, Julie is a sought-after guest expert for print, television, and radio media. Her passion lies in helping people to create *radical, positive, and lasting change* through her coaching, training, and corporate programs – all provided by her company, Leverage U. Julie's home base is the city of St. Catharines, Ontario, where she resides with her husband and their toy poodle.

Books by Julie Christiansen

Anger Solutions: Proven Strategies for Effectively Resolving Anger and Taking Control of Your Emotions

Anger Solutions by the Book: Biblical Principles for Resolving Anger

Bullying is Not a Game: A Parents' Survival Guide (with Laurie Flasko)

It is Well: A Study of Motherhood in Times of Crisis

Leadership AIM (with Executive Coach Global)

When the Last Straw Falls: 30 Ways to Keep Stress from Breaking Your Back

Anger Solutions at Work (E-Book only)

Radical Positive Lasting Change (E-Book only)

Getting Past Your Past (Audio program with Workbook)

Coming Soon! The Rise of Rage (January 2024)

Bibliography

Bible, Adam. (2021). Sha'Carri Richardson Suspended for One Month after Positive THC Test. *MensJournal.com.* https://www.mensjournal.com/sports/shacarri-richardson-suspension-speaks-volumes-of-mental-health-in-sports/

Bauman, S., & Del Rio, A. (2006). Preservice teachers' responses to bullying scenarios: Comparing physical, verbal, and relational bullying. *Journal of Educational Psychology, 98*(1), 219–231. https://doi.org/10.1037/0022-0663.98.1.219

Christiansen, J. (2003). *Anger Solutions: Proven Strategies for Effectively Resolving Anger and Taking Control of Your Emotions.* St. Catharines: Leverage U Press.

Christiansen, J. (2012). *Anger Solutions by the Book: Biblical Principles for Resolving Anger.* St. Catharines: Leverage U Press.

Craig, W. & Pepler, D. J. (1997). Observations of bullying and victimization in the schoolyard. Canadian Journal of School Psychology,13, 41-60. Retrieved from https://www.frfp.ca/bullying-statistics/

Fernandez, Valentina. (2022) Social Media, Dopamine, and Stress: Converging Pathways, Neuroscience, 22X. Retrieved from https://sites.dartmouth.edu/dujs/2022/08/20/social-media-dopamine-and-stress-converging-pathways/

Flasko, L., Christiansen, J. (2012). Bullying is Not a Game: A Parents' Survival Guide. St. Catharines: Leverage U Press.

Gleeson, S. (2021). Naomi Osaka says, 'it's OK to not be OK': standing up for mental health 'all worth it'. *USAToday.com*. https://www.usatoday.com/story/sports/tennis/2021/07/08/naomi-osaka-opens-up-french-open-withdrawal-mental-health/7899251002/

Jacobsen, K., Bauman, S. (2007). Bullying in Schools: School counsellors' responses to three types of bullying incidents. *Professional School Counseling, Vol. 11, Issue 1.*

Osaka, N. (2021). Naomi Osaka: It's O.K. to Not Be O.K. *Time.com*. https://time.com/6077128/naomi-osaka-essay-tokyo-olympics/

Reeve, E. (2021). Simone Biles and 'the twisties': How fear affects the mental health and physical safety of gymnasts. *CNN.com*. Retrieved from: https://www.cnn.com/2021/07/28/us/simone-biles-olympics-gymnastics-physical-mental-health/index.html

Seigel, D.J., Bryson, T.P. (2011). *The Whole Brain Child: 12 Revolutionary Strategies to Nurture Your Child's Developing Mind.* New York: Bantam Books.

Endnotes

1. UNDER PRESSURE

1. Definition of FAITH – *Webster's Dictionary for Everyday Use.* (1986). Miami: PSI & Associates, Inc.
2. Definition of TRUST – *Webster's Dictionary.* (1986).

2. EMOTIONS CAN BE MESSY

1. Genesis 4:8
2. Job 2:11-13
3. Job 2:9
4. 1 Samuel 28:7-15
5. Psalm 61:2
6. Psalm 23:4
7. Mark 14:72
8. Matthew 27:3-5
9. Galatians 3:1
10. 2 Samuel 6:20
11. 2 Samuel 13:19-20
12. 2 Samuel 13:32

3. YOU HAVE CHOICES

1. Joshua 24:15
2. Acts 2:40
3. Philippians 2:12
4. Revelation 3:20
5. Deuteronomy 30:19

6. NOT GOOD ENOUGH – SELF-ESTEEM

1. Narcissism is defined by Dictionary.com as selfishness, involving a sense of entitlement, a lack of empathy, and a need for admiration, as characterizing a personality type.

2. Egocentrism is defined by Dictionary.com as thinking only of oneself, without regard for the feelings or desires of others; self-centered.
3. Fernandez, Valentina. (2022) Social Media, Dopamine, and Stress: Converging Pathways, Neuroscience, 22X. Retrieved from https://sites.dart mouth.edu/dujs/2022/08/20/social-media-dopamine-and-stress-converg ing-pathways/

9. ANGER AT INJUSTICE

1. Retrieved from Stanford Prison Experiment | History & Facts | Britannica

12. LOSS, SADNESS AND GRIEF

1. Adapted from https://www.washington.edu/counseling/resources-for-students/healthy-grieving/#:~:text=Grieving%20such%20losses%20is%20im portant,re%2Dinvest%20that%20energy%20elsewhere.&text=Healthy% 20grieving%20results%20in%20an,peace%2C%20rather%20than%20sear ing%20pain.)

15. OUCH! RESPONDING TO HURTFUL WORDS

1. Craig, W. & Pepler, D. J. (1997). Observations of bullying and victimization in the schoolyard. Canadian Journal of School Psychology,13, 41-60. Retrieved from https://www.frfp.ca/bullying-statistics/
2. Craig & Pepler, 1997.
3. Bauman, S., & Del Rio, A. (2006). Preservice teachers' responses to bullying scenarios: Comparing physical, verbal, and relational bullying. *Journal of Educational Psychology, 98*(1), 219–231. https://doi.org/10.1037/0022-0663.98.1.219
4. Jacobsen, K., Bauman, S. (2007). Bullying in Schools: School counsellors' responses to three types of bullying incidents. *Professional School Counseling, Vol. 11, Issue 1.*
5. Jacobsen and Bauman, 2007.

16. DEPRESSION AND THE SPIRIT OF HEAVINESS

1. Romans 12:2 And be not conformed to this world: but be ye transformed by the renewing of your mind, that ye may prove what is that good, and acceptable, and perfect, will of God.

17. GUILT AND SHAME

1. Psalms 34:18 The LORD is nigh unto them that are of a broken heart; and saveth such as be of a contrite spirit.

   Psalms 51:17 The sacrifices of God are a broken spirit: a broken and a contrite heart, O God, thou wilt not despise.
2. Hebrews 12:2 Looking unto Jesus the author and finisher of our faith; who for the joy that was set before him endured the cross, despising the shame, and is set down at the right hand of the throne of God.
3. Proverbs 3:5 Trust in the Lord with all thine heart, and lean not unto thine own understanding.

18. THE TRUTH ABOUT RELATIONSHIPS

1. Source: Healthy Boundaries handout from Therapist Aid, www.therapistaid.com.
2. "Defining Your Non-Negotiables: This material was adapted from original material by the late Thomas Leonard, the founder of Coachville and Coach U.

19. TAKING RESPONSE-ABILITY FOR YOUR BIG FEELINGS

1. Matthew 26:49 and 50
2. Matthew 6:14-15 For if ye forgive men their trespasses, your heavenly Father will also forgive you:But if ye forgive not men their trespasses, neither will your Father forgive your trespasses. Matthew 18:35 So likewise shall my heavenly Father do also unto you, if ye from your hearts forgive not every one his brother their trespasses.
3. Matthew 16:18 And I say also unto thee, That thou art Peter, and upon this rock I will build my church; and the gates of hell shall not prevail against it.